DETROIT'S STREET RAILWAYS

Volume I: City Lines 1863-1922

D1451872

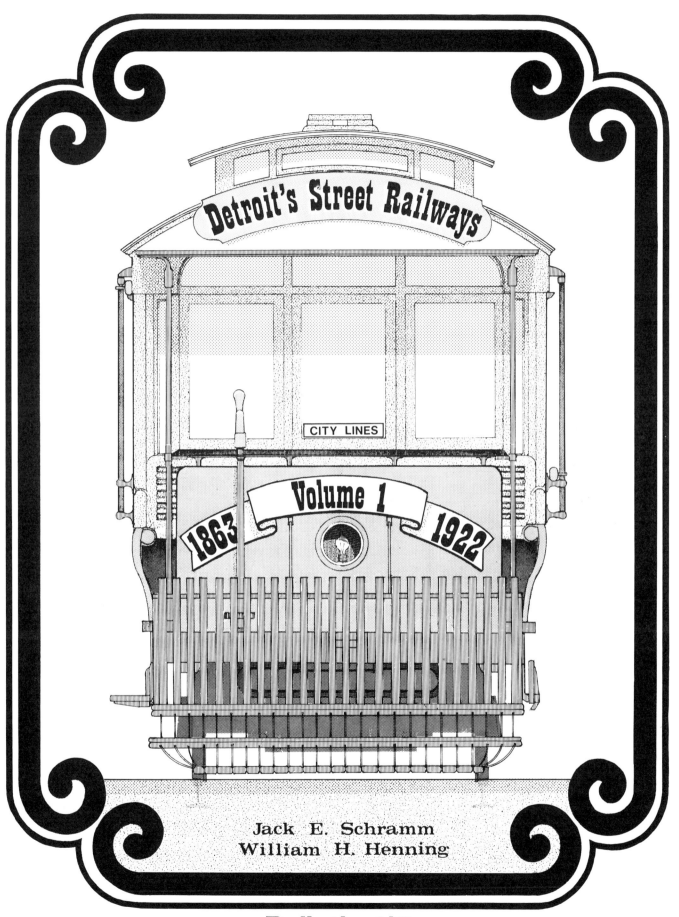

Detroit's Street Railways

CITY LINES

1863 Volume 1 1922

Jack E. Schramm
William H. Henning

Bulletin 117
Central Electric Railfans' Association

Detroit's Street Railways
Volume I: City Lines 1863-1922

Bulletin 117 of Central Electric Railfans' Association

MAR 2 4 1986

Copyright © 1978
by Central Electric Railfans' Association
All rights reserved
An Illinois Not-for-profit Corporation
Post Office Box 503 Chicago, Illinois 60690 USA

Library of Congress Catalog Card No. 77-82927
International Standard Book Number 0-915348-17-9

AUTHORS:
Jack E. Schramm, William H. Henning

ROSTER:
Jack E. Schramm

EDITORIAL STAFF:
Richard R. Andrews, Thomas Dworman

CERA PUBLICATIONS MANAGER
Norman Carlson

COVER DESIGN:
Alexander Pollack

CARTOGRAPHY
Max A. Zink, Stephen M. Scalzo

CERA Bulletins are technical, educational references prepared as historical projects by members of Central Electric Railfans' Association, working without salary in the interest of the subject as a hobby. This Bulletin is consistent with the stated purpose of the corporation: To foster the study of the history, equipment and operation of electric railways. If you the reader can provide any unknown information or are of the opinion that certain information is incorrect please send your information, documented by source material where possible, to: Curator of Corrections, Central Electric Railfans' Association, P.O. Box 503, Chicago, Illinois 60690. U.S.A.

Detroit's Street Railways Volume I was designed by Jack E. Schramm and assembled by Mercedes M. Wetzel and Gallant Graphics, Inc., of Chicago, Illinois. Halftones are by Jim Walter Graphic Arts of Beloit, Wisconsin. The book was printed by Photopress, Inc., Broadview, Illinois and was bound by John F. Cuneo Company, Melrose Park, Illinois.

Acknowledgements

We wish to thank the following people for their extra effort and assistance in locating material for this book: Sherry Balis in the Transportation Library at the University of Michigan, Alice Dalligan and Joseph Oldenberg from the Burton Historical Collection in the Detroit Public Library, and Robert Kothe of the Detroit Historical Museum. For photographic assistance in producing exceptional rare prints, we recognize Joseph Klima, Jr. of the Detroit Institute of Arts, Mr. and Mrs. Manning of Manning Brothers Historical Collection and Harry J. Wolfe. For editorial assistance, we must thank Thomas Dworman, Richard Andrews, and Norman Carlson. We also wish to thank Max Zink and Stephen Scalzo for their help in preparing the maps. Our dust jacket is the work of Alex Pollack who certainly deserves recognition.

Another group of contributors that must be acknowledged are the men, women and relatives who were employed by the Department of Street Railways that contributed historical data, anecdotes and photographs. Also, we want to thank the many traction fans who, through the years, collected and saved many photos from the D.U.R. and D.S.R.files, which were long ago discarded like the streetcars.

Stock certificates, tickets and transfers not individually credited were provided from the personal collections of Richard Andrews and Jack Schramm. For an excellent job in typing the manuscript, we must mention Ms. Suzanne Christy. Charles Petcher was most helpful in reviewing historical data throughout the book. Above all, we must thank two wives who let their husbands devote much time to this project, Barbara A. Schramm and Lois Ann Henning.

JACK E. SCHRAMM
WILLIAM H. HENNING

Detroit, Michigan
December, 1977

Introduction

Electric rail transportation in the State of Michigan was last covered in book form when, in 1959, CERA published "The Electric Railways of Michigan." Detroit's street railway history was only briefly outlined in that book; therefore, this new series should interest persons who want a more detailed history of the Detroit system.

This volume covers street railways in Detroit from their historical inception in 1863 to municipalization in 1922. Detroit, a city of heavy industrial development, was not always a major city. Its history dates back to French and British rule when it started as a trading post, then a sleepy town situated on the Detroit River. It grew rapidly until the early twentieth century, becoming a Great Lakes port and automobile manufacturing capital of the world.

Social changes were being promoted in this growing industrial city by men of wealth who turned politician. As a result, politics played an important part in the city transportation system. Detroit has been described by some as a city that was "planned to death" as each person or group had a "better idea" on how and where the mass transit system should operate. After failure to obtain the famous three cent fare, Mayor Pingree began the long battle to gain city control. In 1922, his successors succeeded. Detroit became America's first large city to own and operate its mass transit system.

Lineage of the predecessor companies, their leaders, politics and social impact on the City of Detroit is studied. Many of the early corporations overlapped, merged or went out of business. Some companies were products of political tactics. Therefore, after analyzing the development of the Detroit trolley corporations, it was decided that its story could best be told by dividing this volume into selected periods of time. Development of the city and suburban system until 1900 is discussed first. Between 1901 and 1920, the Detroit United Railway conducted its operations without competition except for its running battle with city hall. Then in 1920, the City of Detroit built and began to operate a small competing street railway that was commonly referred to as the "Municipal Operation."

Rare pictures taken through the years illustrate the streetcar era in Detroit. The roster of equipment and maps detail the equipment and routes operated by the various companies. Memorabilia completes the presentation.

The complete work should be of interest to historians, rail enthusiasts and the general public alike, thus fulfilling the purpose of this volume as a general reference work on the early history of the Detroit street railway era. Subsequent volumes in this series will detail the history and operation of the Department of Street Railways from 1922 and the interurban railways that were operated by the Detroit United Railway.

Contents

ABOVE: Detroit's Michigan Avenue in the 1870's looking west from downtown. **Burton Historical Collection Detroit Public Library. BELOW:** This photo captured the transition between City Halls. The one on the left was built in 1835 and torn down in 1872. The new building was built in 1872. **Manning Brothers Historical Collection.**

Chapter 1 — Before Detroit United Railway

THE EARLY YEARS 1863-1875

Early Detroit was a boom town with settlers arriving daily. Between the years from 1820 to 1830 the village beside the Detroit River increased by three hundred sixty percent. This population explosion was a result of Detroit being a port of call for travelers continuing their trip west from the newly completed Erie Canal which opened in 1825 in New York State. By 1838 a railroad began operating west from Detroit as a part of Michigan's internal improvement program. Near the mid 1840's the population of the city reached thirteen thousand. Each ten year period thereafter the city's population doubled. Detroit streets became congested with slow moving traffic which caused business men to note that other large urban centers were moving people around town in what was termed mass transit.

Detroit, with one short stretch of paved cobblestone street, had only horsedrawn cabs and buses that connected hotels with railroad stations and boat docks. It was not until 1847 that an attempt was made to develop a bus route along Detroit's East Jefferson Avenue. After a few false starts the system received public support. Detroit, keeping in step with the times, placed its horse bus on rails in 1863. And thirty years later the horse was replaced by the electric motor as a Detroit man popularized it nationally. Investor after investor developed street railway systems in Detroit and elsewhere. In all, a total of eleven separate companies built track systems in Detroit before the century came to an end creating a seemingly complex entangled network of rails and corporations.

THE FIRST OMNIBUS

In May, 1847, Jonas H. Titus began running an omnibus service over a two mile route along East Jefferson Avenue. He offered a thirty minute service and charged a six cent fare. The line was not a success and soon discontinued service. In 1850, Detroit's population was 20,000 and Messers, Drake and Baldwin re-established service on Jefferson Avenue and added a line on Woodward Avenue from the River to Adams. This venture also failed. In 1853 a third company was formed which was moderately successful, although it changed owners several times.

Among the last owners were George Hendrie and Thomas Cox, both of whom later became prominent in street railway affairs.

PLANK ROADS

The State Legislature in 1848 passed the Plank Road Act. This was an attempt to improve the generally poor road conditions by authorizing construction of a network of plank toll roads. Each builder received a sixty year grant and the following routes were built:

Name of Company	Street	Miles-Length	Number of Toll Gates
Detroit and Pontiac	Woodward	18	3
Detroit and Saline	Michigan	40	8
Detroit and Erin	Gratiot	30	6
Detroit and Howell	Grand River	49	10
Detroit and Grosse Pointe	Jefferson	9	2

The rate of toll, set by State Legislature was measured from the center of Detroit at two cents per mile for a wagon pulled by two horses and one cent if pulled by one horse. The early planks in the roadway were replaced by gravel. However, minimal maintenance of the roadway gravel soon made travel difficult.

As the city expanded outward from its center, the toll roads became major streets inside the expanded city limits. Citizens protested against the private corporations controlling these major roads. During the 1890's the city was forced to purchase the toll road charters, improve the roads and remove the toll, although outside the city limits it was business as usual on the company owned toll roads. The streetcar companies were caught in the middle. They needed a city franchise to operate the cars in the city, and also had to arrange for operating rights along the right of way of the toll road. In most instances the streetcar company had to purchase the toll road to gain the right of way. The toll road companies were carried separately on the books of the Detroit United Railway to the end.

A cash receipt from the Detroit and Erin Plank Road.

Toll gate located on Grand River near the present day West Grand Boulevard. **Burton Historical Collection Detroit Public Library.**

LEGEND OF 1874 MAP OF DETROIT

Lines built by Detroit City Railway ————————— 2⅝

1-Jefferson	August 4, 1863	2¾ miles
2-Woodward	August 27, 1863	3 miles
3-Gratiot	September 12, 1863	1¾ miles
4-Michigan	November 25, 1863	

Line built by Fort Street and Elmwood — — — — — 5½ miles
5-Fort Wayne and Elmwood   September 6, 1865

Line built by Grand River Street Railway ——— · ——— · ——— . 2¾ miles
6-Grand River   October 23, 1868

Line built by Hamtramck Street Railway |||||||||| 1½ miles
7-Hamtramck   September 6, 1869

Line built by Detroit and Grand Trunk Junction Railway - - - - - - - - - - - 3 miles
8-Congress and Baker   December 18, 1873

Line built by Central Market, Cass Avenue, and Third Street Railway • • • • • 3⅛ miles
9-Cass and Third   October 16, 1873

Line built by Russell Street, St. Aubin and Detroit and Milwaukee Junction
Street Railway. ——— · — · ———   November 25, 1874   3 miles
10-Russell

Mileage shown was as of January 20, 1876 as recorded in The Detroit Advertiser and Tribune. It also indicated the Detroit City Railway had 3½ miles of double track. The dates shown are the first date of revenue service.

10

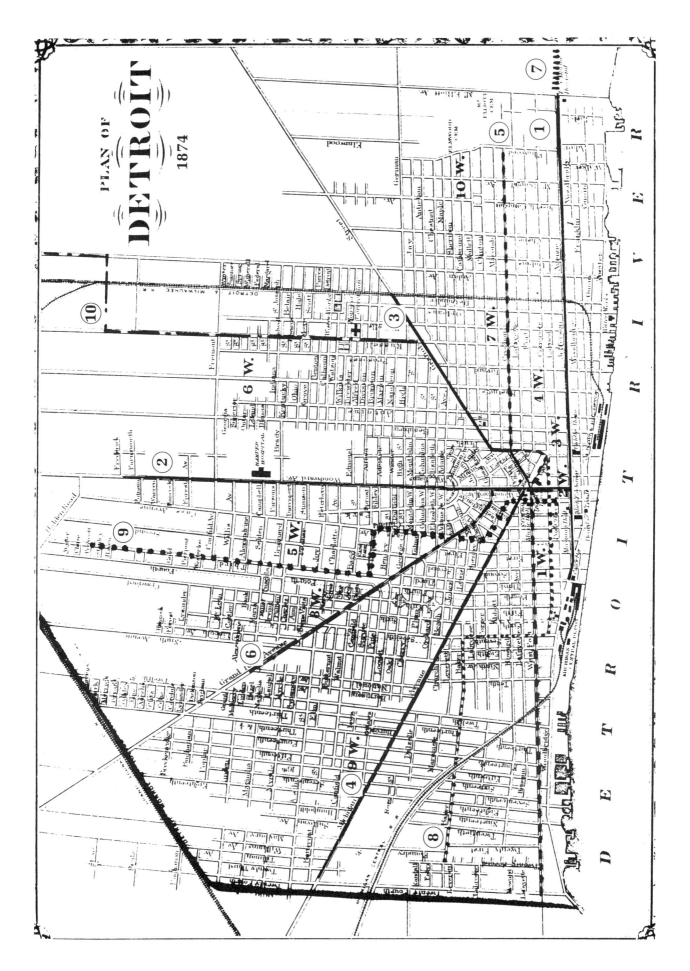

PLAN OF
DETROIT
1874

The citizens of Detroit were justly proud of their City Hall, which was opened July 4, 1871. Photographers used it as a background for many pictures of horsecars and electric streetcars. A Detroit City Railway Woodward Avenue horsecar heads south. **Detroit Historical Museum.**

An unusual photo showing the interior of horsecar 73 restored by the D.S.R. for a parade in 1931. Note the straw on the floor used in winter to warm the passengers feet riding the dark and dreary horsecar. **Manning Bros Historical Collection.**

DETROIT CITY RAILWAY (1863-1890)

By the 1860's narrow crowded streets in Detroit made it necessary to find solutions to moving masses of people about the city quickly and comfortably. The seasonal effect of mud and dust from streets added to the rough ride on streets of cobblestones prompted a search for improvements in the public transit system.

In 1862, Detroit's population was more than 50,000 and the need for expanded public transportation could no longer be ignored. Several major U.S. cities now had horse drawn streetcars, so, on May 24, 1862 the City received a request for a franchise. The required $5,000 deposit was not made and therefore the promoters could not receive from the City the exclusive rights to the streets on which the lines were to be built. The city then advertised for bids to build lines on certain streets with exclusive rights and the first option to build on any additional streets. On November 24, 1862 the council passed an ordinance which designated lines to be built on East Jefferson, Woodward, Michigan, Gratiot, Grand River, and West Fort. Other franchise provisions included definite time limits for construction, nickel fares, hours of service, frequency of service, maximum speed, and a thirty year franchise.

On January 5, 1863, a $5,000 deposit for a franchise was made with the city by a company having financial backers from Syracuse, New York. This group invested $20,000 and sold $100,000 in stocks and $100,000 in bonds locally to build the system. The company was named the Detroit City Railway.

Even though the Civil War still required men and materials, construction commenced that spring on Jefferson Avenue from the Michigan Central Station at Third Street, eastward two miles to Mt. Elliott. On July 31, the Grand Trunk Railroad delivered the first two cars from the car builder in Troy, New York. On August 3, the general public was treated to free rides. Regular service began on August 4, as far as Elmwood Avenue, and by October, to Mt. Elliott Avenue.

The Woodward line began on August 27, and by October was running as far as Alenandrine Street. On September 12, the Gratiot line opened service from downtown to Russell Street, about two miles. By November 25, the Michigan line started operating three track miles to Thompson Street (12th Street) using some of the original Jefferson line streetcars. Jefferson Avenue was considered the prime route, and received the best equipment.

The track guage was an unusual four feet seven inches. This was later changed to the standard four feet eight and one-half inches. The track was constructed with two inch square bar iron spiked to a four foot stringer laid on three inch by eight inch ties, six and one-half feet long and spaced four feet apart.

13

This was laid on a two inch bed of cinders which were placed around the ties and brought up level with the top of the rail. The cinder bed provided good footing for the horses pulling the cars, and for wagons crossing the tracks. In July, 1862 the company established an office on Jefferson Avenue near Woodward. Then in October 1863 they built a car barn to store the cars, at the rear of the Cass Hotel located at Third Street. Previously the cars remained on the streets after they had finished the day's operation.

A short-lived branch line was built along Randolph to Atwater, to Brush, which served the Brush Street Station of the Detroit and Milwaukee Railroad (later Grand Trunk Western). This line became the first abandonment in Detroit when it was removed in April 1865.

The first cars were typical of the sixteen foot horse cars of that era with no heat; only straw was placed on the floor in winter. Interior lighting came from oil lanterns hung in brackets. The cars had platforms on both ends with entry to the interior through sliding doors. A fare of five cents cash or twenty-five tickets for a dollar was charged with no transfer privileges, except at Woodward and Jefferson for passengers going to the railroad depots. A fare increase to six cents was made a few years later when revenue was not up to expectations. City Hall neither approved nor opposed the increased fare.

Three lines used the Woodward track from Jefferson Avenue to Michigan which created a need for route identification. A number of schemes were tried which included painting the route name on the car sides; different colored cars for each line; only one type of car on each line; and a combination of colored signs including the use of various colored lanterns at night.

In the spring of 1864 a transfer station and waiting room for the convenience of passengers was opened. It occupied the second floor of a building on the northwest corner of Woodward and Jefferson Avenues. With newer and larger cars appearing on the streets, the City Council passed a resolution in August 1864 requiring that each car be equiped with a bell to warn pedestrians of the car's approach.

The company's first three years of operation were not profitable. In May, 1866 the system was leased to George Hendrie and Thomas Cox, because it was hoped their combined knowledge of the cartage and bus business could help turn the streetcar system into a profitable venture. Additional shares of stock were authorized increasing the issue from $100,000 to $500,000 to cover the purchase of new equipment and install "T" rail. The nickel fare was re-instated as an additional incentive to attract customers. These measures stabilized the financial condition of the new streetcar company.

Detroit's population was still doubling approximately every ten years. By 1870 the city exceeded 70,000 persons. The necessity for route expansions beyond the construction of the 1860's was evident. A franchise was obtained from Springwells Township, which was beyond the city limits at the time, to extend the Michigan line to the Grand Trunk Junction (at Junction and Federal Streets). To tap this growing area, it was necessary to purchase the right of way of the Detroit and Saline Plank Road Company. Finally on February 23, 1874, the extension was ready. A second fare was charged beyond the city limits of Detroit. In future years this practice was adopted by all companies operating beyond the city limits, which resulted in surrounding communities becoming anxious to be annexed to Detroit for the express purpose of obtaining a single fare.

With the money from the additional stock issue, the line on Jefferson Avenue was double tracked, a turn table was installed at Woodward and Jefferson, and a new large carbarn was built at St. Antoine and Woodbridge. The barn was a block long, 150 feet wide and three stories high, with a connecting track to Jefferson Avenue. This building one of the few early streetcar properties is still standing as of 1976.

In 1876, the Hendrie interests which up to this point only managed the lines, bought the system and operated it until 1891, when pressure for electifing the system caused the successor company to sell out. The Fort line was not built by the Detroit City Railway due to opposition from the people in the affected area. "City" did not build the Grand River Line because it was believed the area had not been built up enough to warrant the investment. Thus the City Railway continued to operate with its four lines during these first years of its existence.

Examples of the early tokens and tickets used during the years George Hendrie leased the Detroit City Railway Company, 1866-1876.

Three examples of the various types of Detroit City Railway horsecars. Notice the window arrangements. **D.S.R. Files.**

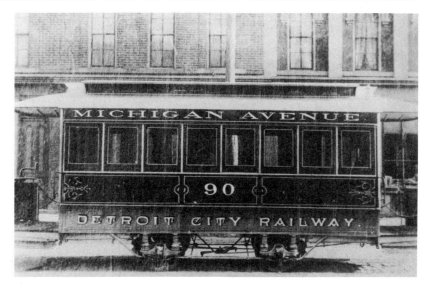

FORT STREET AND ELMWOOD RAILWAY COMPANY (1865-1871)

When the Detroit City Railway forfeited the franchise on Fort Street, a new company was formed calling itself the Fort Street and Elmwood Railway Company, also known as the Fort Street and Elmwood Avenue Railway. The first name appeared on their stock while the second in the thirty year franchise received on January 31, 1865. They received a route on Fort Street from the western city limits near Livernois Avenue running eastward through the Campus Martius and out Crogan Street (Monroe) to Elmwood Cemetery near the eastern city limits. This was the first line to offer rides across the city for a single fare. There was a stock issue of $100,000 of which $70,000 was sold in the first few hours. The articles of incorporation were filed on February 9, 1865 and construction started the following June near 7th Street.

The roadway from downtown to 5th Street was Nicholson pavement with grooves in the block surface for the iron rails. The balance of the west side had planking with grooves for the rails. In August, the first four cars arrived from Gould & Company of Albany, New York. The west side portion of the route began service on September 6, 1865. The following year saw extensions built to both ends of the line so that by September 20, 1866, the line was in full operation from the River Road (West Jefferson) at the Detroit-Sandwich ferry dock, across the city to Elmwood Cemetery at Crogan and Elmwood.

The original barn was built on Clark Street near the River Road on land donated to get streetcar service

down Clark. It had a blacksmith shop and space for ten cars. A new barn was built at the east end of the line which also contained a waiting room and offices. New cars arrived from Worchester, Massachusetts, and Troy, New York, bringing the total number to eleven passenger cars and one construction car.

The line on the west side was further extended to the Fort Wayne military reservation and some double tracking occurred in 1869. The company was a success and their outstanding debt was retired in two years. At that time the capitalization was increased to $130,000. The average per day earnings of a car was $18.38; expenses averaged $13.71 including a daily wage of $4.90. Fares ranged from five to ten cents depending on the distance, with five cent limits in the city.

FORT WAYNE AND ELMWOOD RAILWAY COMPANY (1871-1892)

By an act of the State Legislature in 1871, the old company received a new name, The Fort Wayne and Elmwood Railway Company. Records regarding the reason for the name change are not available, however the Street Railway Act of 1867, states that street railways incorporated under this act cannot have their franchises revoked by local authorities. Therefore, this act would protect the company from future problems with the City of Detroit, which in later years plagued the Detroit Citizens Street Railway which we assume was not incorporated under this act. This one line operation carried on a successful operation and was the last small independent company to operate in Detroit.

This stock was unusual because the old company name was crossed off by pen after unexplained company name change. A new name was added before the stock was sold.

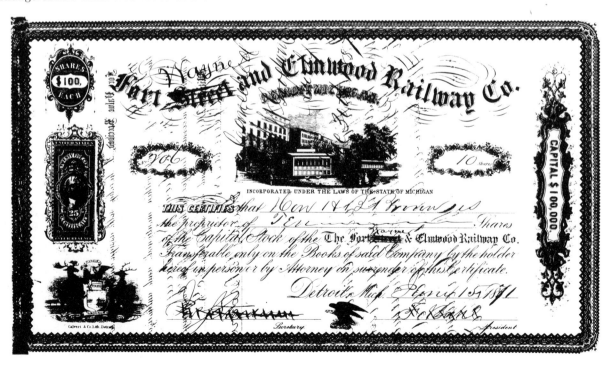

ABOVE: Fort Wayne car 22 stopping in front of the David Scotten Building home of the Hiawatha Tobacco Co. Detroit during these years was a leader in the chewing tobacco industry. This building was built in 1875 at Fort and Campau (Scotten) streets. **Schramm Collection. BELOW:** Car 34 on a winters day on the River Road (West Jefferson) near Livernois. **Burton Historical Collection Detroit Public Library.**

GRAND RIVER STREET RAILWAY (1868-1890)

Detroit City Railway forfeited its rights to the Grand River line on the premise the area was not built up sufficiently. However, the area residents did not agree and demanded service. On May 1, 1868, a franchise was granted to the Grand River Street Railway. Construction started late that month with the first piece of track laid at Grand River and First Street.

The Detroit City Railway sought an injunction to prevent the Grand River Company from laying any additional track on Woodward as the grant provided. The court ruled in favor of the new company and allowed them to build a third track on Woodward west of the existing Detroit City Railway tracks from Grand River to Fort and eventually to Jefferson.

On October 23rd the line began operating. It soon was carrying 30,000 passengers per week and the weekly earnings averaged $310.00.

Slowly the line was extended out Grand River so that by 1875 it reached the city limits then located at the Grand Trunk Railroad crossing west of 16th Street. Fare was a nickel or twenty-four tickets for a dollar. In 1883 the grant was amended to allow a fourth track on Woodward Avenue of which two were four feet seven inches (Detroit City) and two were four feet eight and one-half inches (Grand River).

HAMTRAMCK STREET RAILWAY (1869-1881)

The present-day city of Hamtramck is only a remnant of what was once a much larger Hamtramck Township. In the eastern part of that township near Jefferson Avenue was a popular racetrack. Today, it would be in the Indian Village section of Detroit, near Burns and Jefferson Avenues.

On August 29, 1868 some promoters decided to build a horsecar line on Jefferson from the end of the Detroit City Railway's Jefferson line at Mt. Elliott Street out Jefferson Avenue to the track. They obtained the necessary agreement with the Hamtramck Township Board and called the new line the Hamtramck Street Railway. The grant stipulated that two miles of the line had to be in operation by September 1, 1890 and was a perpetual franchise. Other requirements included a nickel fare, with another five cents charged for up to twenty pounds of personal baggage. Cars were run a minimum of ten hours a day, and provide service at least every thirty minutes. Freight could be carried in cars designed for that purpose.

Strange as it seems the line was incorporated on May 1, 1869 and issued $10,000 in stock after service had begun on September 6, 1868. From its connection with the city line at Mt. Elliott the new company line extended service to the race track. Two Cleveland-built cars operated on the mile and one-quarter track.

THE CENTRAL MARKET, CASS AVENUE AND THIRD STREET RAILWAY (1873-1877)

A request for a franchise to serve the rapidly growing area west of Woodward Avenue was made in September, 1871, under the name of the Griswold Street and Cass Avenue Railway. However, the property owners on Cass Avenue objected and the idea was dropped.

A new group was formed and on June 13, 1873, a franchise was granted over the Mayor's veto. Mayor Moffat vetoed the franchise due to the narrow streets the cars would use. Also he felt the new line was no improvement over the Grand River line in serving the northern portion of Detroit. The franchise was for thirty years with an annual license fee of $12.50 for a one-horse car and $25.00 for a two-horse car. The gross receipts tax schedule called for 1% after five years and 3% thereafter.

Thomas Cox, former partner of George Hendrie, was appointed manager. Construction started near the City Hall on September 26, 1873. By October 16th, cars were running from Griswold and Larned via Griswold, State, Cass, Ledyard to Third, up Third to a terminus near the Holden Road. One of the main loading points was the Post Office at Larned and Griswold and there was usually a car waiting in front of the building. By February of 1874, the eight McCary and Claflim, Cleveland-built cars were carrying 1,000 passengers daily.

DETROIT AND GRAND TRUNK JUNCTION STREET RAILWAY (1873-1875)

On June 13, 1873, a second grant was given by the City Council over the Mayor's veto. He was not in favor of the company's intention to use narrow Congress Street which was only 200 feet north and paralleled the double track Jefferson car route. The grant was for the usual thirty years and the line was to be another crosstown line running westward from Mt. Elliott and Congress via Congress, Joseph Campau, Larned, Randolph, Congress, 7th, Baker (Bagley), 24th, and Dix to the western city limits.

The company's taxes were similar to the Central Market Railway's. Incorporation took place on June 16, 1873 with capitalization set at $150,000. Construction on the western portion of the route was completed by mid-December. The six cars ordered from McCary and Claflin were in readiness and on December 12th service began on the route from Congress and Randolph to 14th. Bridge construction on Baker over the railroad tracks delayed the extention to 22nd Street for an additional week.

A large barn and shops were built on Baker between 10th and 12th Street. An 1874 report disclosed that construction of the car line's eastern trackage was being hampered by the lack of funds. Stock pledges had assured complete construction of the line. But, the unpaid pledges were now so great that a $46,000 construction bill was delinquent by $18,000.

CONGRESS AND BAKER STREET RAILWAY (1875-1879)

The 1909 Barcroft Appraisal noted the Detroit and Grand Trunk Junction Railway transferred to Fred Carlisle, who in turn transferred to Congress and Baker Street Railway Company. Thus on September 17, 1875 the following year the Congress and Baker Street Railway took over the operation of the line.

This rare photograph of a Central Market, Cass Avenue and Third Street car with the original company name printed on the sides was taken at the end of the line at Griswold and Larned. **Schramm Collection.**

ST. AUBIN STREET RAILWAY (1873-1876)

A franchise was granted on July 9, 1873, for a line to run on St. Aubin Avenue from Gratiot to the north city limits of Detroit. However, the franchise was amended changing its route and northern terminal to connect with a busy railroad point which is still known as Milwaukee Junction. Located near St. Aubin and Clay Avenue were the Grand Trunk Western Railroad and Conrail intersect.

The franchise called for a nickel fare, and a license fee of $12.50 for a one-horse or $25.00 for a two-horse car. The city gross receipts tax of 1% after five years and 3% thereafter applied. Actual construction started on July 17, 1874 and by November 25th the cars were in operation. Cars of the St. Aubin Railway used the Detroit City Railway's Woodward and Gratiot trackage before reaching their own rails at Gratiot and Russell. This was the first time that more than one company used the same track.

Some 1875 references to this line listed its name as the Russell Street, St. Aubin Avenue and Detroit & Milwaukee Junction Street Railway Company. It's not known if the company name was lettered on the carsides or not, but if they were, it must have been quite a sight!

The City Railway would not build on Grand River because it would not be profitable. But the citizens on the Avenue demanded a car line; therefore, a new company was formed for that purpose. Notice the serenity of Grand River in those early days. **Burton Historical Collection Detroit Public Library.**

BELOW: The major shopping street of Detroit, Woodward Avenue north of Campus Martius, had three tracks in the center of the street. Both the City's Woodward line and the competing Grand River company shared the street. **Burton Historical Collection Detroit Public Library.**

ABOVE: Woodward Avenue above Campus Martius. The double track of the City Railway became a single track with two tracks as far as Grand River and one track beyond. **Schramm Collection. BELOW:** Early lower Woodward at Jefferson. The Grand River Railway track was at the left and the City Railway at the right with both ending at Jefferson at this time. **Burton Historical Collection Detroit Public Library.**

DAYS OF THE HORSE NUMBERED "SOMETHING BETTER NEEDED"

On October 25, 1872, an epidemic of epizootic, the dreaded horse disease, struck Detroit. No horse cars were in service for several days. This epidemic assisted in pointing out the need for developing other means of propulsion. On December 6, 1872, Mr. A. Wilder demonstrated a "steam dummy". The reason for the term "dummy" was so-called because it was built to simulate a streetcar by disguising the engine's mechanical parts so as not to frighten the horses. This was accomplished by use of a 4-wheel steam locomotive covered by a wood shell simulating a horse car.

An account of the demonstration appeared in the Detroit Union December 7, 1872, as follows:

"About five o'clock yesterday an experimental trial run of a dummy steam engine drawing a streetcar made a trip on Jefferson Avenue. It proceeded about the pace a person could walk until it reached the ascent of the avenue where the twelve passengers had to leave the attached car and assisted in pushing it up the hill. It proceeded as far as Shelby Street and returned, the steam having been exhausted. It does not seem to be improvement over the horse power. The engine was invented by A.A. Wilder of this city and was built by the San Jose and Santa Clara Railway of California".

More trials were reported, but apparently they were not too successful because after a short time no more was heard of the engine.

This ornate car called "Wilders Patent" was an early unsuccessful attempt to replace the horse. Photo was taken in front of the gate of Fort Wayne on Detroit's southwest side on Fort Wayne and Elmwood Railway Trackage. **Burton Historical Collection Detroit Public Library.**

At the beginning of this era, revenues were small and business poor. As the service became more dependable and the lines were extended business increased and revenues began to climb. The streetcar became an important instrument in the development of the city as noted by the Detroit City Council records in May, 1876. They commented as follows;

"The street railways of late have contributed greatly to the development of the city's prosperity. They have enabled the man of small income to live far away from his employment or business at a cheap rent or in a cheap house and for a nominal fee be carried to and from his business or occupation at all hours of day or night. They are a means of building up and improving the outer portion of the city and converting farm land into valuable property".

The streetcar era had begun in earnest.

GEORGE HENDRIE

Real estate developers were quick to place "For Sale" signs on platted land along new streetcar routes. The streetcar like this Woodward car passing Endicott Street increased the property values miles from the heart of the city. **Burton Historical Collection Detroit Public Library.**

PERIOD OF CONSOLIDATION (1876-1885)

Mergers of the various operations in Detroit occurred in the period 1876-1885. Detroit City Railway with its four lines was not only the city's largest system but controlled, what was becoming increasingly apparent as the city grew, the best routes in the city. It was not long before the Detroit City Railway was taking over the smaller companies' trackage and adding to their own system.

In September, 1876, the Russell Street, St. Aubin Avenue and Detroit & Milwaukee Junction Railway was sold to the Detroit City Railway. This short lived operation began in 1873 and evidently was not operating very long after this sale as it was reported not operating the following January. Later that year portions of trackage was taken up and used by the City Railway to double track the Michigan line. The remaining trackage was removed late in 1878 because it was a hazard to the street traffic. The number of companies now were six.

On Saturday, October 28, 1876, fearing an injunction prohibiting construction of a new line to serve the Michigan Central Depot, the Central Market, Cass Avenue and Third Street Railway gathered a large work force at the corner of Griswold and Larned. Before the courts opened on Monday, trackage on Larned Street extending six blocks to the Michigan Central Railroad Third Street Depot was constructed. This new line provided competition to the Jefferson route and the Detroit City Railway Company protested that it was not given first option to build this line as specified in their 1862 grant. Early in 1877, Mayor Lewis informed the City Council he was upholding the Detroit City Railway's position and returning the amended ordinance to the Central Market, Cass Avenue and Third Street Railway. In May of that year they were in the hands of receivers for failure to pay interest on their bond. On May 14, 1877, the name was changed to the Cass Avenue Railway Company.

That August the cars, tracks, and franchises were sold under mortgage foreclosure to George Hendrie for $25,000. The receiver retained the property and barns. Two years later on November 14, 1879 the original grant was withdrawn and it was placed under the original 1862 Detroit City Railway grant. Detroit now had five companies.

Again, in May 1876, City Hall's negative attitude toward streetcar line extension by an independent company resulted in the merger with the Detroit City System. The Congress and Baker Street Railway desired to extend their projected route to Mt. Elliott Avenue as provided for in their original franchise. They wanted to use two streets, Fort and Congress, in a loop operation to eliminate passing tracks and the resulting delays caused by single track operation. The City Council denied their request on the basis that such a loop would confuse visitors to Detroit wanting to catch cars on this line.

The minutes of the Directors Meeting on March 10, 1879 noted that the company was still considering a westward extention through Baker Street (Vernor) to Lovers' Lane (Junction) if enough "bonuses" to pay for the iron could be obtained from the property owners. Many street railway companies received construction funds in the form of bonuses from property owners along the proposed route as an incentive to pass by their land. In this case the funds were never raised and the extention never built.

On November 14, 1879, the Congress and Baker Street Railway had their operating grant withdrawn the same as the Cass Avenue Railway. The Congress and Baker Street Railway Board of Directors, on June 26, 1882 effected a stock transfer on a share for share basis with the Detroit City Railway. The company secretary at the meeting was George Hendrie indicating that when the operating grant was withdrawn in 1879 the Congress and Baker Street Railway was soon under the control of the Detroit City Railway. Detroit now had four companies left.

Hamtramck Street Railway Company became the next victim of a merger as all its operating rights were given to the Detroit City Railway Company by the Hamtramck Township about November 1, 1881. Immediately the new owners changed the track gauge to the Detroit City Railway four feet seven inches and for the first time cars on the Jefferson line ran all the way through from the Michigan Central Depot to the race track. Only three railway companies were left; Detroit City, Fort Wayne and Elmwood and Grand River.

Detroit City Railway received a new thirty year franchise in 1879 which extended its operating rights until 1909. This new grant incorporated the rights previously granted to Congress and Baker Street and the Cass Avenue Railway companies. Some of the new terms of this new grant would become important during the bitter struggles of the 1890's.

One of the provisions of the new grant was a 1% gross earnings tax in place of the license fee. In addition the streetcar company was obliged to furnish the materials and bear all labor costs on the streets with tracks that were to be paved, repaved, or otherwise repaired. Another provision included rebuilding trackage to the Brush Street Depot, by extending the Congress and Baker line down Randolph to Atwater.

While Detroit City Railway was absorbing the other companies, Fort Wayne and Elmwood Railway and Grand River Street Railway remained in operation as independent companies. A new thirty year franchise was granted to Fort Wayne and Elmwood on June 30, 1880. This company continued to operate eleven cars over the original six miles of track. No track extensions were contemplated or mentioned in the franchise renewal. Two years later, the company received a number of new cars from Brill in Philadelphia costing $750.00 each. Grand River Railway served its customers without creating newspaper headlines. It was now a three mile line and had six cars and fifty-five horses. A new franchise was received on December 3, 1885 which contained no mention of additional trackage.

Car 82 after the City Railway took over the Congress and Baker line in 1882. **D.S.R. Files. BELOW:** On April 9, 1872, the Soldiers and Sailors Monument was dedicated. It was built as a memorial to the men who had served in the Civil War. The last four figures placed on the third tier from the bottom section were added on July 19, 1881, dating this photo prior to that period. The large building behind the monument is the Russell House then one of Detroit's foremost hotels located across from City Hall in the center of downtown. A Michigan Avenue line car turning on to Woodward in the foreground. **Burton Historical Collection Detroit Public Library.**

LEFT: The Central Market, built on the site of an earlier City Hall, was opened September 11, 1880. The upper floors were used by various city departments and courts. A Fort Wayne car passes on the right. **BELOW:** A Detroit City Railway car going out Michigan Avenue. The early shoe store on the corner was replaced first by Sanders and later by the Majestic Building, and presently the First Federal Savings. **Schramm Collection. ADJACENT PAGE:** Map illustrates lines operated in 1885 following the period of consolidation:

Detroit City Ry.
————————

Ft. Wayne & Elmwood Ry.
— — — — —

Grand River St. Ry.
—·—·—·—·

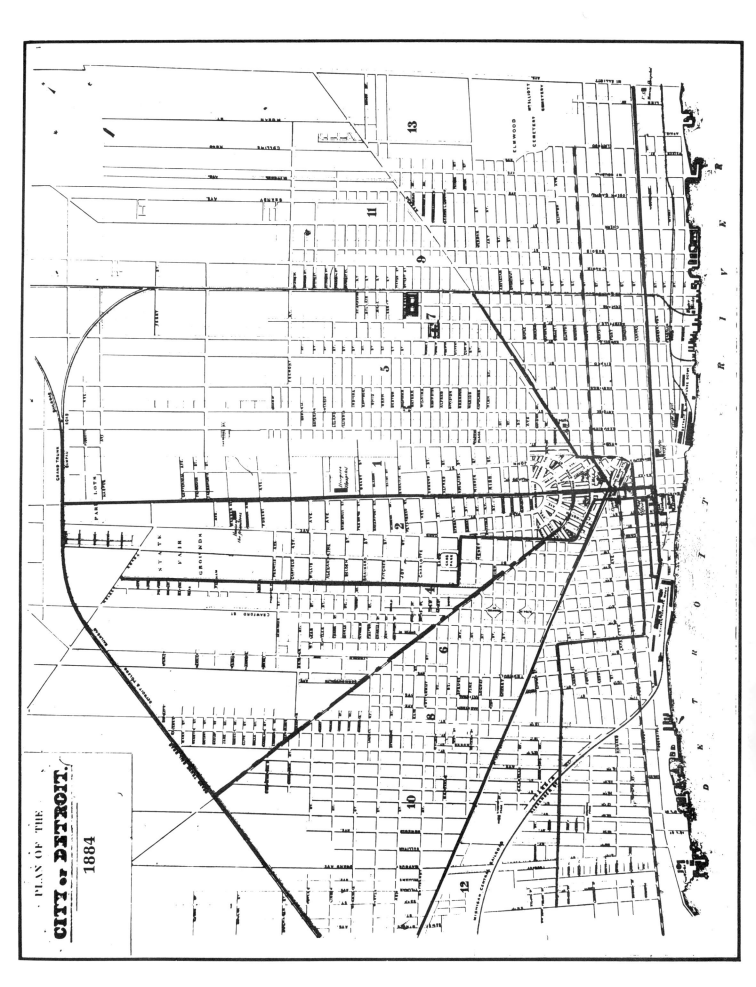

PLAN OF THE
CITY OF DETROIT.
1884

27

Detroit City Railway's regular fare was five cents or twelve tickets for fifty cents. Drivers were permitted to make change up to two dollars, said change being in a sealed envelope. The only mention of transfers was made in an article in the "Farmers Guide" which stated;

"If persons wish to go from either depot by way of Gratiot, Woodward or Michigan lines, if asked for it is the duty of the driver to give a change-off ticket good on the Jefferson route to or from either depot. But a change-off when going from the depot cannot be used going to the depot or vise-versa".

A two horse streetcar plods Woodward Avenue passing the Wright, Kay and Company store which occupied this corner for many years. **Burton Historical Collection Detroit Public Library.**

The Woodward line was extended by 1879 to the Michigan Central Railroad Bay City branch (Baltimore Avenue) crossing. These two photos show the rural appearance of the area which is just a few blocks from the present day world headquarters of the General Motors and Burroughs Corporations. The horsecar had a turntable to reverse direction of travel. At this crossing in later years, passengers could either board the steam train or cross the tracks to the waiting room of the Highland Park Railway electric cars to continue their journey north to the village of Highland Park. **Burton Historical Collection Detroit Public Library.**

ABOVE: The open bench car is going out Michigan passing the early Sanders Pavillion. Mr. Sanders began business at this location in 1875. He was the first to introduce the widely popular "ice cream soda water" in the United States. **BELOW:** An early Detroit City Railway open bench car sitting in front of the Jefferson Avenue shops. **Schramm Collection.**

The Fort Wayne line was now operating from the Boulevard on the east side across the city to Fort Wayne on the west side. **Schramm Collection.**

ABOVE: The early companies operated individual routes from the suburbs. An exception was the Fort Wayne and Elmwood Railway's crosstown route. The popularity of their route may be seen in this crowded car probably taking everyone to the Exposition grounds in Delray. **RIGHT:** Open platforms and foul weather produced this muddy scene. The conductor wore a uniform, but the driver wore a muddy slicker. **BELOW:** In 1892 a west bound car has just crossed Woodward Avenue, while Hansom cabs stand next to City Hall. **All photos Burton Historical Collection Detroit Public Library.**

In 1883 the Grand River Railway franchise was amended to allow four tracks on Woodward from Grand River to Fort Street. Note the light tower in front of City Hall on this wintery day. **Schramm Collection.**

ABOVE: As the population of Detroit topped 116,000 in the 1880's merchants, businessmen, and the transportation system prepared for a swell in economic growth. The Russell House, a prominent hotel, stood ready to receive guests from around the world. The stage was set to allow Detroit to develop into a manufacturing center. In the period from 1880 to 1890 the city rose from 19 to 16 in importance in value of goods produced. **Burton Historical Collection Detroit Public Library. BELOW:** This photo shows the small horse cars moving up Monroe. The dark streaks on the surface could be either water or oil to control dust. Before the days of the electric streetcars it was the responsibility of the city to control dust. **Schramm Collection.**

PERIOD OF EXPANSION (1886-1896)

Two opposing forces surfaced during this period of expansion which left Detroit in a political mess that tended to create rider discontent. Capitalists wanted to invest in streetcar lines in Detroit, as the city continued to grow at a fantastic rate. This population explosion moved the edge of the city outwards. Horsecar lines tried to keep up with the homeseekers as lines were extended to the new neighborhoods, but they began to realize that the economical use of the horse had come to an end. A new solution was needed for a fast cheap people mover. Investors tried various methods but most ideas were not successful, until the discovery of the use of electric power to propel the streetcar.

The advantages of electric power over horse power were numerous: The horse's life expectancy was very short in street railway service, the horse was susceptible to disease, the horse droppings polluted the streets, and most important, the horse traveled very slow. With the advent of electrical power, a great deal of investment was needed; power houses, new heavy track, power lines, new cars and the funds to purchase the equipment costing millions of dollars. Most of the franchises were about to expire, therefore, renewals were needed if the streetcar company was to secure the heavy investment necessary to implement the conversion from horse to electric power.

The 1889 candidate for Mayor, Hazen S. Pingree, was a Detroit businessman whose company manufactured shoes and boots. His establishment was considered a large and successful enterprise. But somehow social reform crept into his thinking and he embarked on a reformist crusade. He and the Hendries parted friendship. Also, other prominent businessmen became the blunt of His Honor's attacks. If railways were to make money in Detroit it would be on his terms; if not, he would start a new company to compete with them even if the city had to operate it. Shortly after his election victory, he challenged the streetcar companies' fare policy. The average citizen was poor and wherever the iniquities were against the citizen Pingree rode forth as a story book knight on a horse slaying the enemy. From his election in 1889 until he was elected governor in 1896, Pingree attacked capitalism. Interestingly it was just before his rise to power that capital investment had been committed to Detroit's street railway systems. Let us retrace the events from 1885 through the expansion period.

During this busy period, the requests for franchises were numerous. One was granted for a projected line which was never constructed on Belle Isle, an island park in the Detroit River. But, a number of new routes were completed by existing companies, several extensions constructed, a new company was formed, and there were some name changes.

GRAND RIVER STREET RAILWAY (1868-1890)

On June 1, 1868, Grand River Street Railway inaugurated service on some new trackage which included the Myrtle line. Later, tracks on Third Street from the Michigan Central Depot to Grand River Avenue were completed in 1889. In cooperation with the Detroit City Railway, they also built a loop line using East Fort Street and East Congress Street from Woodward to Mt. Elliott. George Hendrie acquired the line mid-1888 for a reported $275,000. Hendrie controlled companies usually issued large amounts of stock so on August 4, 1888 the capital stock was increased from $50,000 to $100,000. Then on January 17, 1890, the company was transferred to the Grand River Railway Company. Less than two years later the system was acquired by Detroit Citizens Street Railway Company a successor to the Detroit City Railway for $1,000,000.

Waiting at the end of the line on a summer day, open bench car 28 sits at Woodward and Jefferson. **Burton Historical Collection Detroit Public Library.**

A Grand River car with the large number five on the rear platform turns off Grand River on to Woodward along side a Detroit City Railway Woodward car. Both were heading toward the River. **Burton Historical Collection Detroit Public Library.**

TOP: Car 30 of the Grand River Street Railway Company shortly before the take-over by the Detroit Citizens Railway Company. **Schramm Collection.** CENTER: Downtown Detroit at Campus Martius on the Grand River line during the age of the bustle. **Burton Historical Collection Detroit Public Library.** BOTTOM: Drivers and conductors of the Grand River line. **Schramm Collection.**

DETROIT CITY RAILWAY

The city's largest and oldest railway was very busy between 1885 and 1890 adding a number of new lines and extensions, plus acquiring additional equipment. In a surprise move, starting in June of 1889, the odd four feet seven inch gauge was changed to four feet, eight and one half inches, the same as the rest of the city. Immediately the city wanted the removal of two of the four tracks on Woodward from Grand River to Jefferson. The city felt this was creating undue hazards to the other traffic, especially after all four tracks now belonged to the same company.

The fifth franchise for an electric line within the Detroit area was granted January 3, 1889, (see suburban section Chapter 2, for the previous lines). That same summer the Detroit City Railway began installing an electric system on Mack Avenue which was a new line included in the grant. The city line was to run from Gratiot eastward to a junction with the East Detroit and Grosse Pointe Railway (suburban) which continued out Mack from Cadillac Boulevard, st Ste. Clare Street (now St. Clair in Grosse Pointe) to Jefferson where a large club house was located. The new line did not meet with City Council approval so they ordered the poles removed. The local residents went so far as to cut down the poles already erected and women even sat on the edge of the holes stopping the further installation of poles. The company went to court to get this interference stopped, and by the time the courts handed down a favorable decision, the company lost interest in the project. No further attempts at electrifying the city lines were made until 1892 by a successor company. By September, 1890, the Mack line was being operated by the suburban East Detroit and Grosse Pointe Railway, using a slotted third rail system. They quickly abandoned their tracks on Cadillac Boulevard from Mack to Jefferson and made connections with the Mack line.

On December 1, 1890, the Detroit City Railway was transferred to the Detroit Street Railway.

DETROIT STREET RAILWAY (1890-1891)

This new company wanted to obtain new franchises and convert to electric operation. Within five months, George Hendries newly formed company had labor difficulties. The wages of the car men varied from $1.55 to $1.85 for a twelve hour day. This was changed to $.18 per trip, requiring nine to fifteen trips per day. The weekly pay never exceeded more than $12.25. A number of men at the Detroit Street Railway were discharged when they attempted to organize a union. The city car men fighting for a ten hour day were joined by the men from the Grand River Railway who were discharged for unionist activities on that line. This touched off a strike which erupted into a riot with a number of cars overturned and burned. The strike began April 21, 1891, and ended on April 24th. Arbitration settled most issues, but the decisive item was recognition of the union. Also an agreement was reached on May 12th, that provided a wage rate of $.18 per hour, and a ten hour day for conductors, and $1.50 per day for drivers.

The company's request for a thirty year franchise, which included a cable car line for Woodward, was approved by the City Council on June 23, 1891. However, Mayor Pingree returned it without his approval two weeks later, stating he was against the private ownership of a natural monopoly. Further, he felt that the original franchise granted in 1862 would expire in 1892, and the projected 1909 dates were invalid. He advocated either selling the franchise to reduce taxes or reducing the fare. In a special Council meeting on July 9, 1891, Pingree's action was upheld 18-0. This signaled a change in the relationship between the city and the streetcar companies. With their bid for a new franchise having been denied, the Detroit Street Railway was transferred to the Detroit Citizens Street Railway on September 16, 1891.

DETROIT CITIZENS STREET RAILWAY (1891-1900)

The "Citizens" as this new company was popularly called issued stock in the amount of $4,000.000 of which $3,000,000 was used to acquire the Detroit Street Railway and the remaining $1,000,000 was to purchase the Grand River Railway Company. The new operators agreed to 50% electrification within a two-year period. On April 5, 1892, they notified the Board of Public Works that they wished to begin converting a section of the Jefferson line to electric operation. Contracts were let for ten additional cars to be purchased from the Jones Company for $10,000. These, and two cars already on the property were to be outfitted with 40-horsepower motors obtained from the Detroit Electrical Works. In June, work was begun even though the City had not approved the project, and by August 22, 1892, the line was ready.

The following is from the Detroit Tribune, August 23, 1892:

"It was just 7:42 o'clock yesterday morning when the first electrical car rumbled out of the power house at St. Antoine and Woodbridge Streets and began to climb laboriously up the little incline to Jefferson Avenue. On board were officials of the Company and the Detroit Electrical Works. There was some difficulty in getting up the incline. Once the car ran off the tracks; however at last the avenue was reached. Once on Jefferson, the car moved easily speeding at a rapid rate. Working men passing along the street stopped and waved their hats. People living along the route arose from their breakfast tables and came out on porches with their napkins in hands and shook them at the passing car. At the barns (at Bellevue) the car stopped to pick up more officials including George Russell (company treasurer) who had come in on the suburban car out Jefferson. The car went to Baldwin and returned downtown. The second, third, and fourth cars were started an hour apart, the operators were instructed by experts from the Detroit Electric Works. By the end of the first day there were seven cars moving up and down the line; however, they took no passengers the first day".

The article also reported that on August 23, regular service would begin using not more than eight of the twelve cars equiped with the electric motors. The new cars should make the trip from Woodward to the Beltline railroad crossing at Beaufait in about half an hour, half the time of the horse car.

Car suppliers like G.E., Westinghouse, Detroit Electric Works, bid for the new business. Detroit Electric Works received the bulk of the Woodward line order. Conversion of the Woodward line to the electric system was completed in mid-December, which was followed by the Mack line. Early in 1893, all-night service was begun on the Woodward and Jefferson lines. In September of that year the Woodward line was extended into Highland Park when the Highland Park Railway (suburban) was given a grant to cross the Grand Trunk and Michigan Central tracks near Baltimore and connect with the Citizens line. With these three lines completed further conversions ceased due in part to franchise questions which were being litigated.

In May, 1893, Judge Taft of the U.S. Circuit Court ruled the franchise extensions null and void. The Citizens appealed his ruling to the U.S. Court of Appeals which reversed the lower court's ruling stating that the franchise was in fact legal and binding until 1909. On November 12, 1893, the Michigan Supreme Court refused to hear Mayor Pingree's plea for an additional ruling.

J.D. Hawks, general manager of the Citizens was negotiating with a special committee from the Council to arrive at an out-of-court settlement. The company wanted to extend its franchises until September 16, 1921, on all lines. In return they agreed to electrify within three years, and universal transfers. During the summer of 1894, Alderman Vernor and the Council worked out a tentative franchise. It was vetoed by the Mayor and the veto was upheld by Council 17 to 13.

In face of this defeat the Detroit investors who controlled the Citizens, sold their interests to R.T. Wilson, of New York City for a reported $.75 on the $1.00. The holding company for this new venture called itself the Detroit Traction Company, otherwise it was business as usual. Tom Johnson of Cleveland became a partner with Wilson having purchased 1/5 interest in the venture and had the title of President. Jere C. Hutchins was hired and quickly named Vice-President and Acting Manager.

Hutchins promptly set about electrifying the rest of the system. It was Hutchins who later was to become the guiding genius of the Detroit United Railway. In his book "A Personal Story", he describes the Grand River electrification as follows:

"We were in mid-winter but seeing an opportunity to begin the policy of converting the horse car line to electric by the purchase of fifteen cars which had been built for another company, we made the purchase. We dug through the frost for a pole line of Grand River, hired some power from the old Detroit Electric Works, took off the horses, and started the electric line on Grand River on the ninth day of February, 1895, when the thermometer was several degrees below zero".

The cars referred to, came from the Nassau Electric Railroad of Brooklyn, New York. That company was unable to accept them due to the collapse of their power house, and sold them to Detroit. They arrived with the Nassau name lettered on them, and numbered 41-55. By 1899 they had been renumbered 441-455.

Conversion of Grand River to electric power allowed the company to use the Myrtle and Crawford horsecars as trailers when they reached Grand River for the run downtown. In August, the Michigan and Gratiot lines were changed over to electric service. By November, all lines were converted to electric power and on the 9th of that month, the last horse car made its final ceremonial trip. This car carried signs reading "The last horse car", as it traveled from the Citizens Company office to the City Hall, proceeded by playing bands. At City Hall the car was coupled behind an electric car and pulled around the city. When the car arrived back at the barns, people began stripping it for souvenirs.

With the change over to electric power, numerous route changes took place and several crosstown lines were formed. During the summer and fall of 1895, Jefferson and Grand River, and Gratiot and Michigan lines were joined; Chene north of Gratiot was routed downtown via Gratiot and joined with Trumbull. The portion of the line south of Gratiot became the South Chene line; Congress and Baker lines were joined with Dix (suburban) and later the Loop line (on East Fort and East Congress Streets) and renamed Baker. In addition a large number of lines were re-routed and several lines were renamed.

Tom Johnson of the Citizens and Mayor Pingree were at odds constantly over fares. The Mayor insisted on a three cent fare with a free transfer. Johnson claimed the company could not break even, let alone make a profit unless fares were higher or transfers abolished. The fares constantly were being adjusted up and down, at which point the Mayor suggested that the eight for $.25 tickets should be changed to three for $.10, so that the poorer class of workers could take advantage of the lower fares. Johnson discontinued the six for $.25 tickets as a fare and insisted on the five cent fare called for in the franchise. Mayor Pingree tried to be forced off a street car, hoping the issue of being forced to leave would give him good press coverage and then he could sue for damages. The Mayor alighted almost at the point of forceful ejection, but the proclaimed lawsuit was not carried out. In another instance a conductor was suspended for letting the Mayor ride free. Later, a friend paid the fare so as to avoid confrontation with the conductor. The battle over fares raged on and on.

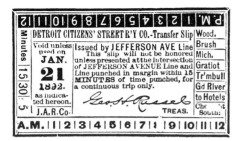

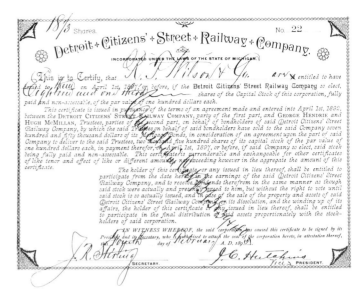

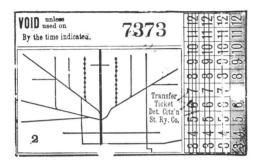

FRONT   **BACK**

ABOVE: This close-up shot of the foot of Woodward at the Detroit River shows the four tracks and the bunching up of cars in this area. BELOW: A view up Woodward from the Ferry Landing taken about 1890. Today, both the ferries and streetcars are gone from the scene and Woodward no longer runs to the river. **Burton Historical Collection Detroit Public Library.**

Detroit's City Hall circle 1888. The occasion for the celebration is unknown but a fair turn out of buggies and people was achieved. **Manning Brothers Historical Collection.**

ABOVE: This mix of horsecars shows the line-up at Woodward and Jefferson. **D.S.R. Files. BELOW:** City Hall was the center of attraction in this 1892 photograph. Both open and closed horse cars were evident shortly before electric cars were introduced in the downtown area. **Schramm Collection.**

ABOVE: 202 on the Chene Line. This line was one of the last horsecar lines in the city. The man with the derby and mustache was the driver; the conductor wore the uniform since he was able to get inside the car out of the weather. **Schramm Collection.**

RIGHT: Conductors and drivers of the Chene Line. Note the drivers were all equipped with whips. **D.U.R. Files. BELOW:** Car 73 in service. In later years after use as a shoe repair shop it was restored by the D.S.R., after trading a Birney body for it. Then after use in a parade in 1931 was allowed to deteriate in the Highland Park yards. **Schramm Collection.**

ABOVE: Car 79 of the Jefferson line just east of Woodward. The city was decked out for another special occasion. **Burton Historical Collection Detroit Public Library. BELOW:** A rainy day as car 24 of the Myrtle line passes Soldiers and Sailors Monument. **Schramm Collection.**

The first electrics on Woodward were built by Pullman. Here mixed with them is a Crawford line horse car. These early electrics still had the open front platform the same as horse cars. **Burton Historical Collection Detroit Public Library.**

An 1890's photo of a horse drawn line wagon showing the uniformed linemen working on the crossing of the overhead on the Detroit Citizen's Woodward line and the Fort Wayne's single line on Fort. **Schramm Collection.**

Track building in the first years of street railways consisted of a roadway for the horses and a run way for wheels of the light weight horsecars. The streets were unpaved and the area around the 2" square rails and ties were filled in with cinders to maintain the grade and give the horses footing.

After 1892 and the use of the heavier electric cars the track construction was done by this three car unit furnished by the Johnson Co. Power for the unit is via a fishing pole which makes a side contact with the trolley wire allowing the streetcars in service to operate on a temporary track. The unit consists of three cars, one a welding car with a crane and hoister at one end, also four water tanks to supply water to keep the contact points from overheating. The second car is a compressor car powered by two 25 H.P. motors, and carries a hydraulic pump used to compress the track to overcome the breaking of the welds in winter. The third car is a flat car with two one H.P. motors needed to operate a emery wheel to grind the welds.

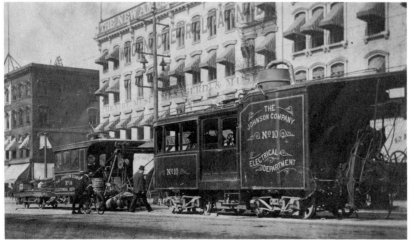

ABOVE: A temporary track is laid to the side of the road using light "T" rail on wooden ties. In earlier days when a track was rebuilt the service was discontinued during the period of reconstruction. **LEFT:** Photo of the three unit Johnson Company track service at Woodward and Jefferson. **Schramm Collection.**

FORT WAYNE AND ELMWOOD RAILWAY (1871-1892)

The single line Fort Street and Elmwood Railway, which had its start in 1865, was Detroit's second street railway company. It remained independent during this period of expansion. Business seemed to be good so the company also invested funds in expanding its lines first westward to Woodmere Cemetery. This extension opened for service October 11, 1886. The following June the line was extended east to East Grand Blvd. Their single crosstown line had little competition from the other lines which required the use of two or more cars and usually two fares to cross the city.

They were granted a franchise in 1889 to construct a line on Champlain (East Lafayette) Street running parallel with Monroe Street, giving service similar to the nearby Loop line. The following year they experimented with a storage battery car over a section of the line. They considered electrifying their line from Woodward to Springwells Avenue in April, 1892. The reason probably being the large crowds carried to the Detroit International Fair and Exposition grounds located near Springwells Avenue on the far southwest side of the city.

FORT WAYNE AND BELLE ISLE RAILWAY (1892-1897)

On July 1, 1892, the rights, franchise, and property of the Fort Wayne and Elmwood Railway were transferred to the Fort Wayne and Belle Isle Railway in a company reorganization. General Electric Company of Chicago was given a contract to equip the entire line with overhead trolley to be completed by the following October 1st. J.C. Brill Company of Philadelphia was given a contract to build thirty, eighteen foot Palace cars. To finance the improvements and new equipment it was necessary to have a new bond issue. The maturity date of these bonds was beyond the 1895 expiration of the original franchise of the Fort Wayne and Elmwood Railway. The new corporate name was a part of this program.

The power house was to be built on a 140 x 150 foot piece of property on Clark Street near the Wabash Railroad. The 1200 horsepower engines to generate power were to be furnished by Allis-Corliss Engline Company of Milwaukee, Wisconsin. Poles for the overhead were to be of the round iron type in the center of town, and to be the octagonal wooden type in the outskirts. The purchase of electrical equipment was financed by issuing $400,000 of improvement bonds. Trial runs were made in mid-October, 1892, then on February 23, 1893, regular service with electric cars began. Within three weeks the last horsecar operated, as the line was fully equiped with electrics. That June they absorbed the Detroit, River Rouge and Dearborn Railway on West Fort Street (suburban) and operated it as part of their line. In 1896 they reported their first loss, due in part to the competition from the other newly formed crosstown lines.

Fort Wayne Working-man ticket.

The Fort Wayne and Elmwood Railway Company car house on Clark. **Barcroft Apprasial.**

Early electrification projects on the Fort Wayne line used horses to pull a homemade wagon. Metal span wire poles were used in the downtown area while wooden octagon poles were popular elsewhere on the system . . . **Burton Historical Collection Detroit Public Library.**

Open bench car 41 of the Fort Wayne line heads west on Fort, while on Woodward heading north a Detroit Citizens horsecar is about to pass a Woodward open bench electric. **Schramm Collection.**

Poor streets, muddy in the spring and dusty in the summer were common in downtown Detroit. The horsecar on rail made all weather transportation possible throughout the city. The Fort Wayne and Elmwood Railway crossing Woodward on Fort Street provided an important through crosstown service.

BELOW: Behind a light tower, one of 72 towers contracted for in 1884, car 540 heads towards the river past the Russell House which had been enlarged in 1876 and was a leading hotel. **Schramm collection.**

A lonely Fort Wayne electric going west on Fort Street. The building with the tower was the Post Office and Federal Building which opened on October 27, 1897. It was located on the north side of Fort between Shelby and Wayne. The building on the extreme left, the Hammond Building, ten stories high, when built in 1889 was one of the first skyscrapers. **Schramm collection.**

The Fort Wayne with its single line became Detroit's first all-electric operation. **Schramm Collection.**

DETROIT MICH.

SHOWING

DETROIT RAILWAY

NOVEMBER 1895.

LINES IN OPERATION.

FRANCHISES NOT BUILT.

PROSPECTIVE FRANCHISES.

DETROIT RAILWAY (1894-1896) The Three Cent Lines.

During January of 1894 when the Citizens and Mayor Pingree could not come to terms on a new franchise, mainly over the matter of fares, Pingree came up with a new idea. He decided to look elsewhere for capital with which to build a system of streetcar lines that would offer a three cent fare. After much delay he was finally able to interest the Pack-Everett syndicate in his venture. On November 21, 1894, Pingree announced that an agreement had been reached and that the new system would be known as the Detroit Railway Company.

In short order a thirty year franchise was drawn up with rights to operate on Warren, Forest, Fourteenth, Hasting, Sherman, Harper, Catherine (Madison) and a number of lesser streets. The fare was eight tickets for $.25 from 5:45 a.m. to 8:00 p.m., and six tickets for $.25 the balance of the day or a cash fare of $.05 and universal transfers at all times. To get these low fares, the city agreed to maintain the tracks — something never before offered. Also the city could purchase the lines at the expiration of the franchise at a price set by arbitration.

In mid-December, the Mayor turned the first spadeful of dirt, signalling the start of construction. Immediately the Citizens Railway went to court to secure an injunction to stop this construction. Their position was that the 1862 grant gave them first option to build on the streets of Detroit. The Circuit Court refused to issue an injunction and the Citizens Railway appealed. While the appeal was being heard, construction on the new system progressed rapidly. Property for barns and power houses were obtained and the franchise to operate in adjacent Greenfield Township was secured. By July 1, 1895, the Detroit Railway began operating a single car over a portion of their lines. On July 8, regular service over the Crosstown & Belle Isle line began, and again Detroit had three operating companies. During October and November the following lines began service: Catherine and Sherman; Fourteenth; Oakland; Belt Lines via Hastings and Fourteenth; Porter; and Ferry Loop. On May 8, 1896, the Mt. Elliott line began operating which was to become part of the Harper line. The long awaited three cent lines were at last a reality, but actually it was $.03⅛ fare only when using tickets.

The first change in operation occurred on October 10, 1895, when the Mayor and Council approved an ordinance granting the Detroit Railway the right to operate on Michigan Avenue using a portion of the Citizens Railway tracks. They were to pay a fee of $10,000 and relinquish its rights to lay tracks on certain narrow streets. A week later Catherine and Sherman cars began looping downtown, using the Citizens eastbound track on Michigan Avenue.

In mid-November, 1895, owl service was begun on three lines. That same Thanksgiving, the ridership went up, due to a fare increase by the competing Citizens Railway.

Seventy of their seventy-six cars were needed to handle the extra traffic. There were more trackage arrangements worked out between the two companies and little by little suspicions grew that this was a prelude to a takeover by the Citizens. The rumors persisted and it became evident that it was just a matter of time until the two systems merged. In his book, Tom Johnson, President of the Citizens Railway, wrote;

"The city gave Everett the grant and he built the road. We completed remodeling the old lines before this was done; and when he operated at three cents, we did the same. We didn't need the money. Our enterprise was financed and we could stand the contest. Everett had yet to raise the money for his project. It was a foregone conclusion that with our better laid out system our lines at first would cripple, then acquire the three cent road".

Mayor Pingree understandably was disturbed and then angry as the plans for the consolidation became apparent. It had been his plan from the beginning that the Detroit Railway would defeat the Citizens, but just the opposite seemed to be happening. He immediately sought legal opinions to prevent the impending merger. It became known that some stockholders held shares in both companies, and he was told that there was nothing to prevent the stockholders of one company to purchase shares in another company with a merger or consolidation as the end result. On July 29, 1896, the Detroit Railway was sold to the Detroit Electric Railway.

During this period of expansion the number of operating companies were reduced to two and then, increased to three with several name changes sandwiched in between. Horse cars had given away to all-electric operation and the matter of fares raged endlessly.

The next period of Detroit's traction history will witness the formation of a one-company, city wide operation with Tom Johnson as the head of the system.

STATE OF MICHIGAN.

No. A21   SHARES $100.00 EACH.   —100 Shares.

THE DETROIT RAILWAY.

This is to Certify, that N. A. Everett, Cleveland, Ohio
is entitled to One Hundred ———shares of the Capital Stock of
THE DETROIT RAILWAY,
transferable only on the books of the Company by the holder hereof, in person or by attorney on the surrender of this Certificate.

Vice

IN WITNESS WHEREOF, the President and Secretary have hereunto set their
hands and affixed the seal of the Company, at Detroit, Michigan, this
Twentieth day of May 1895

Secretary.   Vice President.

Two photos taken on the first day of operation of the Detroit Railway Company on July 8, 1895 with 22 miles of track completed. The motorman on the first car in the train was Mayor Pingree. **Schramm collection.**

A page taken from the booklet printed by the Detroit Railway in 1896. **Burton Historical Collection Detroit Public Library.**

Warren Car House 1896. **Schramm collection.**

The City was developing its suburban area by promoting rapid transit to downtown. The photo upper left taken at Medbury Grand and Beubien shows the undeveloped area just inside the city limits. **CENTER:** Car 84 loading at Capital Park, downtown Detroit. **BELOW:** Car 8 of the Sherman line. Cars arrived every few minutes in the heart of the city providing cheap fast service. **Burton Historical Collection Detroit Public Library.**

THE DETROIT ELECTRIC RAILWAY (1896-1900)

This was the second company to use the name, The Detroit Electric Railway. The first was the short lived Detroit Electric Railway, which operated an electric line on Dix Avenue in 1886 (see suburban section).

This new company was capitalized with one million dollars in common stock and bonds outstanding at $2,800,000. The holders of Detroit Railway stock exchanged their shares at par for bonds in the new company and the remainder of the bonds ($1,800,000) were used to replace the old Detroit Railway bonds.

The new Detroit Electric Railway stated that the only change in the affairs of the company was in the name as they needed to increase the mortgage bonds by a million dollars to build suburban lines. Mayor Pingree insisted that the sale was out of order on the basis that a provision in the franchise of the old company prohibited its sale to the other company. He feared the outright takeover of the new company by the Citizen interests. His fears were strengthened, when on September 16, 1896, the Detroit Electric closed its power house and purchased power from the Citizens company. On the heels of this, it next closed its repair facilities, and the rival line planned to repair all cars until it found out the wider Detroit Railway cars would not fit into the Citizens shops. Where upon, the Detroit Electric reopened the Warren Car House to repair the cars.

By January 4, 1897, the Citizens Company officers were in full control of the Detroit Electric Railway, and only the three cent fares distinguished their lines from the rest. Tom Johnson attempted to purchase stock until he had controlling interest, but before that happened the Directors of The Detroit Electric Railway asked J.C. Hutchins of the Citizens to take over the management of the system. On that same date, the Citizens Company gained control of the Fort Wayne and Belle Isle Railway Company which on April 1, 1898, became the Detroit, Fort Wayne and Belle Isle Railway. Now the Citizens management had control of all the important street railways in Detroit. They formed the Citizens Traction Company in 1897 as the holding company with the intention of consolidating all the streetcar lines in Detroit. With the lines under one control they next set out to make improvements in the system. A number of re-routings were made to eliminate overlapping or competing routes. A great deal of unneeded trackage in the downtown area was removed. The fares were six tickets for $.25 except on the three cent lines.

In 1897, the company introduced a couple of special car services. First, an official car named the DuPont, numbered 88, was outfitted for use by railway officials when on inspection or other official trips. Next placed in service was a funeral car, which was formerly car number 1 of the Detroit Railway. It was rebuilt with upholstering throughout, a special compartment for the casket, and seating for thirty persons. The first trip was to Woodmere Cemetery with the body of a former streetcar conductor. The funeral car was followed by four regular cars draped in black.

Later another type of service was proposed. The Detroit postmaster returned from Washington with a plan to operate post-office cars. Three cars would be built and roam the city on a radius of five miles from the center of town. Five pickups per day were planned from special mail boxes. The City objected to this plan claiming it would slow up service and create traffic tie-ups, so the plan was dropped. Late that same year, the Council adopted an ordinance regulating the car speed to ten miles per hour in the inner city and fifteen miles per hour farther out.

Still advocating municipal ownership of the street car lines, Mayor Pingree was elected Governor of Michigan in 1897. He attempted to be both Governor of the state and Mayor at the same time, until the courts made him finally vacate the latter office. Johnson and Pingree ceased being antagonists even to Johnson being quoted as stating;

"The next time His Honor Pingree plans to be bounced from a streetcar, to let him know, so he can be conductor as it would only be fitting for His Honor to be bounced by the President of the Road".

The article also noted Pingree received on old Myrtle horse car as a relic. It was delivered March 14, 1897 by Manager DuPont. Pingree placed the car in the backyard as a playhouse for his children. He even had a three-cent fare sign placed on the car.

On December 13, 1898, J.C. Hutchins of the Citizens appeared before the Detroit Committee on Streets and Ordinances to present the company's position on a new franchise. In return for a thirty year franchise renewal, the company would agree to the following: Six for $.25 fares including free transfers, pay for paving between the tracks, pay 2% of its gross earnings to the city, consider the lines under the original township grants as extensions of the system, one-half hour extension of the workingmans tickets in the evening, build new trackage and extensions to existing lines, and in cases where street widening was necessary, to permit double tracking, the company would pay for the widening and first paving. Alderman Beamer of Detroit termed the offer an "insult" (only city ownership would do) and it was turned down by an overwhelming 30-3 vote. He further promised that a bill would soon be introduced into the State Legislature to authorize the city to build and operate its own system. Jere Hutchins, Vice-President of the Citizens, related in his book that since Pingree was now in the Governor's Office he was not interested in pursuing the three cent fare issue. But, Tom Johnson by now had become involved in a new political philosophy that saw the government owning the trolley system. He and Pingree met in private and arranged a plan whereby the stage would be set for municipal ownership.

Early in 1899, Representative McLeod, formerly a streetcar conductor and union representative, introduced a bill in the State Legislature called "An Act to authorize the City of Detroit to construct, acquire, maintain, and operate street railways and to construct extension thereof". On March 24th of that year, the bill was passed, and the next day was signed by Governor Pingree. The first commission was appointed by the City Council with terms ranging from two to six years. The Commission members included Governor Pingree, Elliott Stevenson, a one-time Mayor of Port Huron, Michigan, now a Detroit lawyer with an interest in traction, and Charles Schmidt. Schmidt soon resigned and Hutchins was elected in his place.

On April 3, 1899, the new commission sent the Citizens a letter that they were ready to negotiate for the sale of the railway to the city. The basis for valuation of the system would be reproduction cost. The Citizens Company immediately organized the Metropolitan Railway Company for the purpose of consolidating all the underlying properties and making ready for the negotiations with the city. Two days later they replied to the city that they were ready to discuss terms. E.B. Hutchinson of the Citizens Company was to determine the valuation, and the Commission would have it verified. Prof. E.W. Bemis of the Kansas Agricultural College was selected to check the company's figures. M.E. Cooley, Dean of Engineering, University of Michigan, was to evaluate all property and cars.

However, not everybody was in favor of municipal ownership. Several prominent businessmen, including J.L. Hudson, formed what was called the "Citizens Opposition Committee", which sought a court injunction to restrain the Street Railway Commission's actions. They cited, among their objections, the feared loss of taxes paid to the city by the railway. In 1898, this totaled over $23,000. They also pointed out that the company paid a sizable amount of the paving costs on the streets where the cars ran. They further questioned the city's liability in a case of injury or damage suit due to negligent operation. On April 24, 1899, a bill of complaint was forwarded to the State Railway Commission. Meanwhile, Prof. Bemis was carefully going over the figures submitted by the Citizens Company. In mid-May, Governor Pingree announced that a partial agreement had been reached.

On May 24th, the Commission submitted a report to the Council. In the report, Prof. Bemis verified that the Citizens Company's figures were accurate, the franchises were valued at $8,478,563, and

buildings, tracks, land and equipment at $8,000,000, a grand total of nearly $16,500,000. The Citizens Company was willing to sell out for $15,273,000 in cash. Since the City could only offer 4% bonds secured by the earnings of the road, the owners felt that these bonds would sell for 90% par, and asked $16,800,000 in bonds. They figured the city would actually sell $17,500,000 in bonds and keep the difference as a cash reserve. The Bemis report also included the following inventory of the property;

Track

103.84 miles, Detroit Citizens Street Railway
 25.55 miles, Fort Wayne and Belle Isle Railway
 54.68 miles, The Detroit Electric Railway
184.07 miles total

Car Houses and Shops

Detroit Citizen:	Jefferson car house and shops Woodward, Michigan, Baker, Trumbull, Third, Brush Car Houses
Fort Wayne:	Clark and Helen Car Houses
Detroit Electric:	Warren and Kercheval Car Houses

Rolling Stock

Detroit Citizen:	*223	Closed Car Bodies
	242	Open Car Bodies
	21	Miscellaneous Work Cars
Fort Wayne:	12	Closed Car Bodies
	6	Open Car Bodies
Detroit Electric:	92	Closed Car Bodies
	20	Open Car Bodies
	6	Miscellaneous Work Cars

On June 5, 1899, the Detroit Street Railway Commission placed it's final report before the City Council hoping it would be accepted and that steps would be taken to secure municipal ownership. Commissioner Stevenson, Judge Speed, and Jere Hutchins journeyed to New York to confer with R.T. Wilson, owner of the Citizens Company. They hoped to clear up the remaining points of disagreement in the proposed sale. They hoped he would be willing to grant concessions regarding the security franchise, the length of franchise, and the rates of fare. The meetings were fruitful with the fare question settled at rates of six for $.25. Also, the length of the franchise was to be for thirty years, which could be extended another eighteen years if the City needed it to pay off the obligations.

The new system was to be called the Detroit Municipal Railway. It would issue $17,500,000 in bonds to purchase the physical property and franchises that belonged to a certain corporation known as the Metropolitan Railway Company. This company was in reality the holding company for the Citizens Company. The proposal was put before the Council. They in turn referred it to the Committee on Streets and Ordinances as a delaying tactic, rather than acting on it.

Another powerful opposition group known as the "Citizens Committee of 62" announced that they would withdraw their opposition to municipal operation if the fares were set at three cents instead of five. They felt sure, however, that R.T. Wilson would never agree to such an arrangement. Past history had shown that a three cent fare did not cover the cost of operation. A proposal to place the matter of purchase before the people was shelved on June 27, 1899. Among the reasons given by the Council was the lack of three cent fares, and a fear of litigation if a favorable vote was given by the people.

A few days later, on July 5th, Governor Pingree's hopes of a municipal operation suffered a crushing setback. On that date the Michigan Supreme Court found the McLeod Bill unconstitutional on at least six counts. One of the counts declared that legally there was no such office as the Street Railway Commission. However, the resourceful governor was not through yet. He was determined to keep trying; he felt that for Detroit, Municipal ownership was the only answer. On July 12th, he succeeded in getting the Detroit Common Council into special session with the Street Railway Commission. After this meeting it was announced that articles of incorporation had been filed for a private firm composed of the commissioners to take over and operate the lines until such time as an amendment to the State Constitution would permit direct operation by the City. The new Commission was to consist of Governor Pingree, Elliott Stevenson, and Jere Hutchins. Detroit's Mayor William Mayberry announced his intention to veto the measure. In spite of this, the Council voted 19 to 14 in favor of the interim plan. They approved a six for $.25 fare and a forty-eight year security franchise. This plan was never put into operation because on July 16th, before any action could be taken, Gov. Pingree received a letter from the Metropolitan Railway, terminating negotiations. It stated briefly, they felt that nothing could come of any further talks, and they would continue to operate the system as best they could. The letter ended ten years of continued efforts by Pingree to secure a city owned street railway system. He was no closer to municipal operation now than he had been when first elected Mayor of Detroit in 1889.

In August the Council again tried to force three cent fares on the Citizens by passing an ordinance requiring an eight for $.25 ticket. The company secured an injunction stopping its enforcement and then went to the U.S. Circuit Court to get it permanently set aside. Judge Swan, on March 19, 1900, handed down a decision in favor of the streetcar company.

On September 9th, the Commission made one last attempt to re-open the discussion of the street railway sale with R.T. Wilson in New York. He refused to grant any more options that would tie up his property. Also, the asking price was now up to $17,000,000. For the present it seemed the idea of a municipally operated streetcar system was a dead issue as far as the company was concerned.

This resulted in the City of Detroit increasing the total assessment from $2,600,000 in 1899 to $10,000,000 in 1900, to reflect the values of the franchises, an increase of city tax assessments of $67,871 per year. A local article quoted Tom Johnson as saying he would have rather paid $100,000 than make the information available on franchise values.

Things were fairly quiet for the next fifteen months. Then, on December 30, 1900, several associates of R.T. Wilson including Henry Everett, who had built the three cent lines, arrived in Detroit to announce to the press that all of the streetcar systems in the Detroit area had been consolidated into a new system to be known as the Detroit United Railway. All franchises of the Detroit Electric Railway; Detroit, Fort Wayne and Belle Isle Railway; Detroit Citizens Street Railway; and all remaining trackage of the Detroit Suburban Railway was transferred to the new company. At long last a single company was a reality.

Three photos of the late 1890's. **TOP:** Woodward just north of Jefferson. **CENTER:** the streetcars early competition was the bicycle. Location could have been Bates and Jefferson. **Schramm Collection. BOTTOM:** Jefferson looking east from Griswold. **Burton Historical Collection Detroit Public Library.**

Car 493 lays over at the end of the line near West Grand Blvd. **Courtesy of V. Fischione.**

With the use of the faster electric cars the unpaved dusty summer streets created dirt problems to passenger and resident. The City solved this problem in their usual way by adding a financial burden to the street car companies. June 29, 1897 an ordinance requiring street railway companies to sprinkle between the tracks was passed. This was done instead of paving streets and the watering continued after the streets were paved. The Detroit Railway had electric sprinklers on their line, which were flat cars upon which sat a 12 foot long tank, 6 feet in diameter with a capacity of 2500 gallons. The car required a crew of two. And they could sprinkle six miles of track with each filling. **Schramm collection.** **BELOW:** A later and larger type sprinkler which also was able to help pay the cost by advertising on the sides, in this case company advertisements. **Schramm collection.**

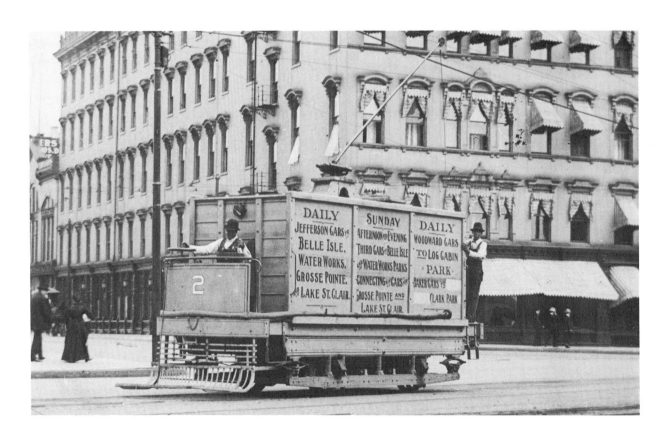

TOP: This car, number 88, had been one of the original Jones cars used on Jefferson. On December 24, 1897, Superintendent Du Pont used number 88 as his private car to inaugurate service to Dearborn. It was rebuilt into an office car with seats removed and outfitted with desk and chair. **Robertson Collection. BELOW:** Many of the early Jones cars were rebuilt into line cars as was 95 shown here. **Faber Collection.**

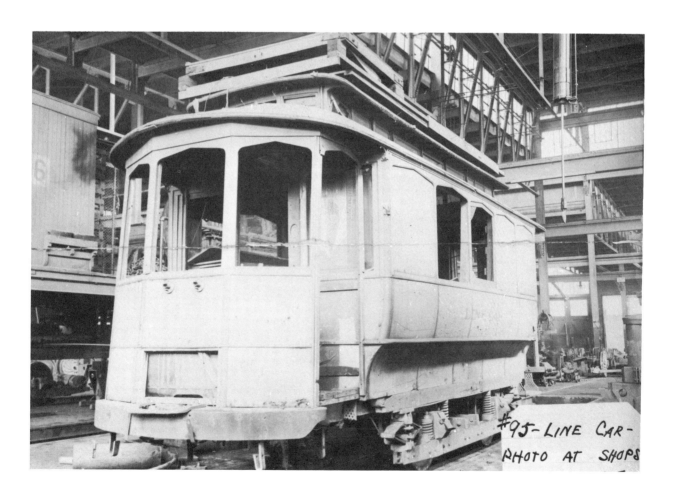

#95-LINE CAR-
PHOTO AT SHOPS

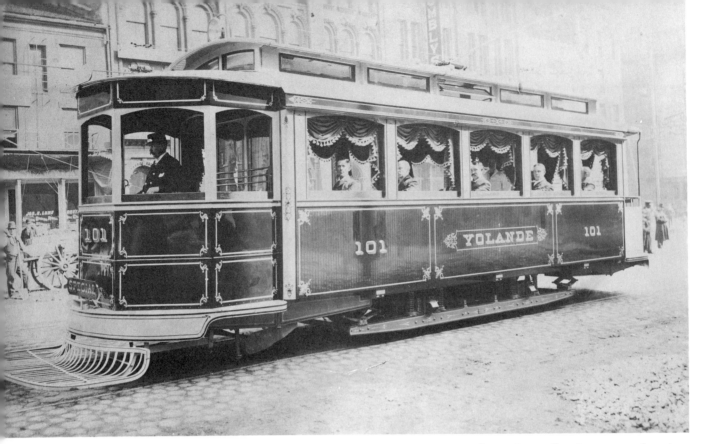

The "Yolande" was the name of the special car of the Detroit Citizens Railway. It was fitted up proper for a tour car, a party car, or a special occasion car. Car 101 held the name until 1902 as shown above, then in 1902 a larger double trucked car replaced it. The name continued with the new car while 101 was placed in passenger service. **Robertson Collection. BELOW:** 101 is in front of the Concord Car House serving the Sherman line. This car was included in the sale to the D.S.R. when it was renumbered 350 and used for tripper service. **Schramm Collection.**

Car 1 of the Detroit Railway inaugurated service for the company. Later it was rebuilt into a funeral car and first used on June 17, 1897 for a funeral at Woodmere Cemetery for the burial of a Citizens Railway motorman. The car lead a black draped train of four other cars. The funeral car was painted black with gold trimming and could carry 28 mourners. **TOP:** first day of operation. **CENTER:** as a funeral car named "Special" **BOTTOM:** Interior of the funeral car showing seating arrangement. **Henning Collection.**

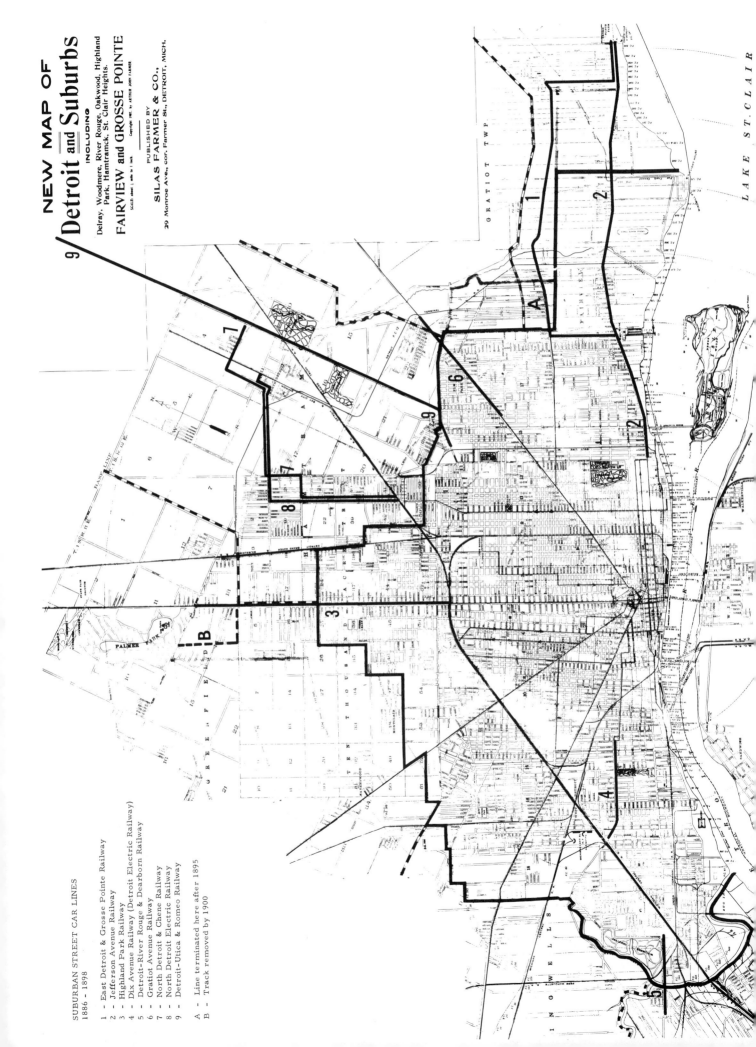

NEW MAP OF
Detroit and Suburbs

INCLUDING

Delray, Woodmere, River Rouge, Oakwood, Highland
Park, Hamtramck, St. Clair Heights.

FAIRVIEW and GROSSE POINTE

SCALE about 1 mile to 1 inch.

Copyright 1897 by ARTHUR JOHN FARMER

PUBLISHED BY

SILAS FARMER & CO.,

20 Monroe Ave., cor. Farmer St., DETROIT, MICH.

SUBURBAN STREET CAR LINES

1886 - 1898

1 - East Detroit & Grosse Pointe Railway
2 - Jefferson Avenue Railway
3 - Highland Park Railway
4 - Dix Avenue Railway (Detroit Electric Railway)
5 - Detroit-River Rouge & Dearborn Railway
6 - Gratiot Avenue Railway
7 - North Detroit & Chene Railway
8 - North Detroit Electric Railway
9 - Detroit-Utica & Romeo Railway

A - Line terminated here after 1895
B - Track removed by 1900

Chapter 2 — Early Suburban Operations

DETROIT SUBURBAN RAILWAY (1892-1900)

Up to 1891 the Detroit city boundary lines covered roughly the area inside the present day Grand Boulevard. Outside of that perimeter was considered the suburbs, where a number of suburban car lines were promoted that would connect with the city lines. Late in 1892 the Detroit Suburban Railway was created to consolidate these independent companies: Jefferson Avenue Railway; East Detroit and Grosse Pointe Railway; Gratiot Avenue Railway; Detroit Electric Railway, (Dix Avenue); Highland Park Railway and the construction of a line on Chene to Norris, (North Detroit). This company, Detroit Suburban Railway, was actually a holding company and as far as is known, never operated any equipment under that name. The following is a description of these lines in order of their first day of operation.

DETROIT ELECTRIC RAILWAY (1886-1892) Detroit's First Electric System

The streetcar propelled by electric power was nearing reality for Detroiters in the mid 1880's. Electric motors were finding new applications almost monthly. Inventors like Wernier Van Siemens in Germany, Stephen D. Field, and Thomas A. Edison from the U.S., all applied for similar patents around 1880, using electricity to transport people. They were to be followed by Leo Daft, John C. Henry, and Bently Knight; but it took Charles J. Van Depoele and Frank Sprague through the sale of their inventions to the public that popularized the electric streetcar. Van Depoele, an immigrant from Belgium, settled in Detroit in 1874 and continued experimenting with electric machines while carrying on a successful manufacture of art furniture. He is credited with lighting Most Holy Trinity Church, Christmas Eve, 1879 which is reported as the first public building lighted by electricity in the United States.

Van Depoele is reported to have discussed using electric power to operate a Detroit Street Railway car, but shortly he moved to Chicago to continue experimenting with electric motors. In February 1883, a 400 foot test track was completed and placed in operation. This test was set-up to sell the plan to the promoters of the new Chicago El. It was not successful. By 1886, and several expositions later, Charles Van Depoele was able to interest several cities in the electric streetcar. Windsor, Ontario, Canada, was the first to purchase the Van Depoele system in the Detroit area. The first electric car in Windsor began operating June 6, 1886. This construction inspired Detroiters to promote a line on Dix Avenue (Vernor), from 24th to the city limits at Livernois and beyond that opened for service September 1, 1886. Port Huron, Michigan, quickly followed with their own Van Depoele line on October 17, 1886.

Generally, real estate developers and speculators became the promoters of electric transportation. In the case of the Dix Avenue line on the west side of Detroit, a real estate developer joined with George Dorr; Calvin K. Branden, investor; Bethune Duffield, lawyer (associated with the Detroit City Railway); and H.C. Campbell, lawyer associated with Michigan Central Railroad, to acquire a franchise to build an electric line. A look at the map of Detroit reveals the area served by the car line had streets named after these men.

On April 17, 1886, a franchise was given to the group who formed the Dix Avenue Railway Company, which almost immediately became the Detroit Electric Railway Company. A grant from Detroit was obtained first, which plotted a line to run from a connection with the Detroit City Railway at 24th and Dix, westward to the city limits. On May 10th, that same year, a franchise from Springwells Township was obtained. This extended the line via Woodmere Cemetery to Fort Street and the present Woodmere Avenue. This Van Depoele installation employed double overhead wires, a motor located on the front platform of the car, and a chain to drive the car wheels. An article printed by the Van Depoele people in 1887 described the installation as follows:

"At Detroit, Michigan a road has been equipped with one motor and generator. This is a new road, one and three quarter miles in length, running out of the city. The cars have been run at a rate of 27 miles per hour. The road was equipped with electrical apparatus by the Van Depoele Construction Company of Detroit. The first trips were made on September 1, 1886. Each motor pulls a train of three cars and runs from 6:00 a.m. to 11:00 p.m. This is what is known as the Dix Road line, and is owned by the Detroit Electric Railway Company. H.M. Campbell is President, and Henry Russell (Detroit City Railway) is secretary. It is run in connection with the Detroit City Railway. The road will shortly be extended to the stockyards. Two additional fifteen horsepower motors are now being put on the new cars. The double overhead wire is being used. Power is taken to run the cars from the generators in the Michigan Central Railroad car shops. The present plant consists of two twenty horse power motor cars, each capable of pulling a train of three cars, and two fifteen horsepower cars".

The cars were also lighted by electricity. The line was giving thirty minute service and efforts were being made to have ten minute headways. At the same time they were to reduce the objectionable noises from the overhead. It was caused by a combination of the rollers skating over the wires and the arcing from poor contact. This problem was never a concern in Port Huron or Windsor. Detroiters were looking for an excuse to reject the line, therefore any noise was cause to complain. On October 10,

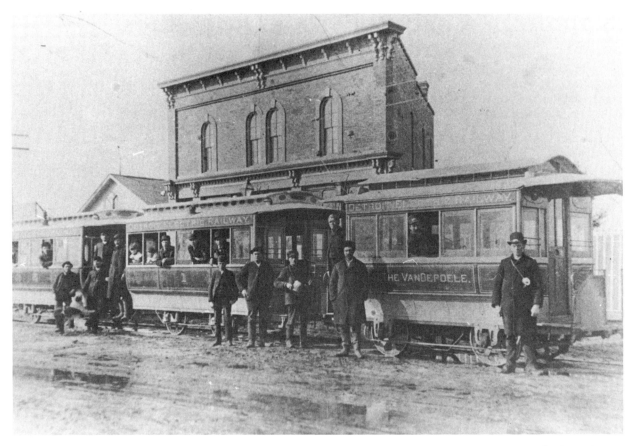

Taken the first day of operation on the Dix Avenue line which was the first electric operation in the Detroit area. **Schramm Collection.**

1888, the City Council sent the company a resolution regarding the line's failure to maintain the scheduled ten minute service. The company replied that it was a new and untried system. It further stated that its performance was improving and that the cost of operation had been reduced to only half that of a horse car system.

Never-the-less, a further resolution by the City Council on May 14, 1889, forbid the company from changing to a single overhead wire with a grounded third rail, which the company had begun to do without formal approval. Two weeks later, the original franchise was revoked. The company was ordered to change to animal power. Among the reasons cited were the still objectionable noises from the overhead, irregular service and the high "T" rail which was considered a traffic hinderance. Therefore, on June 11, 1889, a new franchise requiring horse power went into effect and the line was

changed over before the end of the year, the only thing remaining electric was the name.

The conversion to horse power was costly, therefore the Detroit City Railway was reported to have financed the project. Also, the city company agreed to operate the line on a day-to-day agreement but kept separate books. Passengers transferred at the junction of the two companies. A full $.05 fare was charged for a through ride, the Detroit Electric receiving $.03 and the Citizens, $.02. The Citizens was paying a 10% rental on the cost of the 1889 reconstruction, $2,000 per year. They also, had guaranteed bonds amounting to $15,000 bearing interest of 8%.

The 1889 Poor's Manual listed the rolling stock as six cars and twelve horses. On November 1, 1892, the Detroit Suburban Railway took over this line. The trackage in later years was to become part of the Baker line.

HIGHLAND PARK RAILWAY COMPANY (1885-1893)

Greenfield Township issued a grant on October 17, 1885, for a line to operate "on Woodward Avenue from the railroad crossing of the Grand Trunk Railroad in Detroit to the six mile stake in Highland Park", a distance of five miles. On May 12, 1886, the Highland Park Railway was incorporated and issued $50,000 in capital stock. On July 13, of that year, Detroit issued a franchise to complete the line.

They purchased land at the Grand Trunk Railroad crossing at which point a waiting room was built. This also served as a transfer station for Woodward Avenue cars of the Detroit City Railway. Local fare was a nickel; an eight cent fare was good for a transfer to the Detroit City Railway to the downtown area.

Frank Snow, a real estate developer, also promoter of the East Detroit and Grosse Pointe Railway, was a moving force behind this line. Like the other line, this new venture was of the slotted third rail, or Fisher System. Installation was by the Detroit Electric Works. There were two types of motor mounts on the Pullman built cars. One, the "Ampere" (the cars were named) had the motor mounted under the car. The other, "Faraday", had the motor on the front platform. Each car had a ten horse power motor and could pull a fully loaded trailer. Turning around of the cars was eased by turntables at each end of the line.

Operation began September 18, 1886, thus the line became Detroit's second electric operation. Average speed was eighteen miles per hour over the three and one-half miles that had been built.

The last 100 shares of stock were sold in November, 1889, to finance the conversion from third rail to overhead trolley. The power house was sold to Detroit Electric Works for $42,000, with payment to be made through power usage. Detroit Electric Works used the power plant as part of their expanded foundry site. In 1895 this power plant supplied the needed power when the Citizens was converting to electrical operation on Grand River.

When the Detroit Suburban Railway assumed control on February 1, 1893, they agreed to complete the line as outlined in the original franchise. Almost immediately they ran into problems with Detroit over the location of the tracks in the street. The city wanted to have the Woodward Avenue track relocated to the center of the street (the track had been on the west side of the street). In spite of no agreement, paving proceeded, leaving an unpaved strip down the middle. It was fenced in as a safety measure, and quickly became known as "Pig Lane" by the newspapers at that time. Of course, during this period, all service on the line was suspended. Now problems with Highland Park developed over the service stoppage and eight cent fare. Work on laying track in "Pig Lane" was completed finally, but in spite of this a mob began tearing up the track in Highland Park. It took Jere Hutchins, who had just arrived in Detroit to get the cars rolling again. In June, 1895, a new grant was issued which called for the line to be extended to Palmer Park via Woodward to Kanada Road (near present day Detroit Terminal Railroad Tracks), westerly along a private right-of-way to Hamilton and north to the Casino in Palmer Park. Here, a connection was made with cars of the Oakland Railway to Pontiac. It wasn't until October 2, 1900, that the grant was amended to allow the use of Woodward straight through Highland Park. The line via Hamilton was discontinued and permission given to remove the tracks.

Both Detroit Citizens Railway conductors and Highland Park Railway conductors, issued two types of tickets to through passengers. One ticket was good over both lines to the city limits and sold for $.05, of which the city company received $.035. The other ticket was good between the river and Highland Park, if sold by the city company it retained $.045, and if collected in the fare box, it received $.035.

In 1889, Poor's Manual listed the rolling stock as six electric passenger cars, and four electric motor cars for pulling trailers. By 1892, Street Railway Journal listed eight cars, four single-truck closed cars and four single-truck open cars and of these, four were equipped by the Detroit Electric Works.

The "Ampere" as it originally operated by a third rail system. Later it was converted to a trolley system. **Burton Historical Collection Detroit Public Library.**

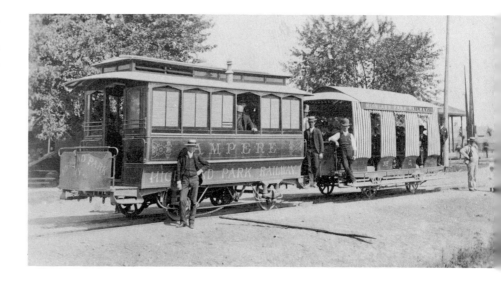

The "Ampere" after conversion to the overhead trolley system. **Schramm Collection. RIGHT:** A rare photo of a Highland Park electric car taken alongside the power plant which was taken over by the Detroit Electric Company. Originally a portion of it was built and operated by the Highland ParkRailway. **Robert E. Lee Collection.**

EAST DETROIT AND GROSSE POINTE RAIL WAY (1887-1892)

Many street railway promoters began by first gathering grants or franchises from the local towns before the company was formed. In some cases the grant once owned, was sold by the promoters to investors. It is suspected the reasons behind the forming of the East Detroit and Grosse Pointe Railway was land promotion. Grants were acquired on March 29, 1887, for operation in Hamtramck Township; and in Grosse Pointe Township on April 11th. By May 11th, a state charter was issued to Calvin Branden (Detroit Electric); Frank Snow, Real Estate promoter; plus others. The line was projected from Jefferson and Cadillac, via Cadillac, Mack, St. Clare, to Jefferson again, to the Club House at Fisher. Since the line was outside the city, electric power was selected, with a local electric manufacturing company providing the Fisher or slotted third rail system of current pick up. The barn and power house was located on Mack Avenue, near Conners Creek. Four cars were purchased and by January 15, 1888, the line was complete.

In May, the cars were running the twelve and one-half mile round trip in twenty-eight minutes. In 1889, the company took over the operation of the Mack line from the Detroit City Railway after they were unable to electrify the line. Since the system used a slotted third rail, it was acceptable to the residents along the route. At this time the track on Cadillac was abandoned and in 1892 was ordered removed by the City Council because this area was now within city limits.

In October, 1891, the original grant was amended to permit the use of the Healy System Motor as motive power. Soon three of these units were in service. The Healy's used either hard coal or coke gas as fuel. The standard motor weighed five tons and was capable of pulling five fully loaded cars. There were eventually seven Healy's in use, spread between this company and the nearby Jefferson Avenue Railway.

The Poor's Manual of 1889, listed the capital stock as $100,000 and the rolling stock consisting of four cars and three electric motors. By 1890, there were eight cars and three electric motors.

On November 1, 1892, the Detroit Suburban Railway took over the company. In 1894, the Mack line was shortened. The portion from Hamilton (Harding) to Grosse Pointe was abandoned. The portion from Hamilton to Gratiot became a city line.

JEFFERSON AVENUE RAILWAY COMPANY (1881-1892)

The old Hamtramck Railway Company which had been taken over by George Hendrie and associates in 1881, was leased to the Detroit City Railway for operation. On May 29, 1886, George Hendrie organized the Hamtramck and Grosse Pointe Railway as a holding company. The 1889 Poor's Manual listed the company as owning two miles of track gauge four feet seven inches, and six cars and twelve horses. By 1890 the gauge was listed as four feet eight and one-half inches. There were two reasons for keeping the

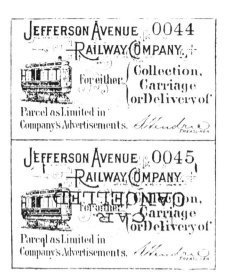

companies separate; the perpetual franchise and the privilege to carry freight.

The village of Grosse Pointe granted rights on March 13, 1881, to the Hamtramck and Grosse Pointe Railway to run a line on Jefferson Avenue from the east to the west village line. They also obtained rights to operate on a private right-of-way along Fisher Avenue, if necessary. At the same time Grosse Pointe Township granted rights to operate on Jefferson Avenue within the township limits.

In May, work was underway and in June the company was formally incorporated as the Jefferson Avenue Railway. A Healy motor (steam dummy) made a number of trial runs that summer from the water works to the country club at Fisher Road. Revenue service commenced on September 7, 1891.

In 1892 Street Railway Review had an article on the express service provided by the Jefferson Avenue Railway. The map indicated the area served began at the Michigan Central Depot and ran eight miles to a summer resort along a thickly populated toll road. The train was drawn by a Healy Motor and consisted of the motor, express car, and passenger car. Mail was carried in locked pouches under a star route contract. There were five stations for receiving and delivering packages. Charges for the service were made by selling stamps by conductors, express managers, and at stations, at ten cents each which were then attached to the parcel.

Prior to the track extension to Grosse Pointe, the lease between the Hamtramck and Grosse Pointe Railway and the Citizen Railway provided for annual rental of $875.00 plus maintaining the tracks and buildings. As soon as the Jefferson Avenue Railway line was complete to Grosse Pointe the lease would cease and both companies would furnish their own cars and operate through service. The Hamtramck and Grosse Pointe was to receive $.015 for each through passenger, and the City $.035. Each company was to receive a milage fee for the use of the others cars, by either company. The company was taken over November 1, 1892, by the Detroit Suburban Railway and the trackage later became part of the Jefferson line.

HEALY STEAM MOTORS

CAN NOW BE SEEN

IN DAILY COMMERCIAL USE IN DETROIT.

NOISELESS, SMOKELESS, NO AUDIBLE EXHAUST.

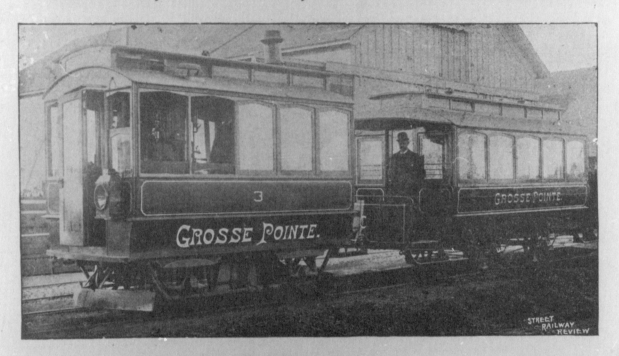

TESTS.

POWER.—— { 241 Passengers were carried on the 25th of August, 1891, in two trailers and motor, two an one-half miles in eighteen minutes, although delayed by horse cars.

SPEED.—— { Four and Seven-Eighths Miles has been repeatedly run by motors in regular service in fifteen minutes.

ECONOMY. { A motor was run about ten hours per day for thirty days in regular Street Railway Service, on the Jefferson Avenue Line of the Detroit Street Railway Company, drawing one or two trailers, as required, making 2,232 miles with an expenditure of 15,780 lbs. of coal and 9,000 lbs. of coke. The cost for coal, coke, wages of motor-man, oil, waste, motor repairs,—in fact the total expense was $113.92, or five and one-tenth cents per car mile.

STOPS.—— { Steam brakes set tight by a turn of the wrist in less than one-fifth of a second.

FOR FURTHER PARTICULARS SEE PAGES 81 TO 84 OF FEBRUARY, 1892, STREET RAILWAY REVIEW.

C. E. HEALY, AGENT.

974 JEFFERSON AVE. · DETROIT, MICH.

TOP: The starting of service on the line with a Healy Motor. The man in the window with the straw hat was Mr. Healy. **Detroit Historical Museum. CENTER** and **BOTTOM:** Two cars of the Hamtramck and Grosse Pointe Railway. **D.S.R. File photos.**

GRATIOT AVENUE RAILWAY COMPANY (1891-1892)

On May 7, 1891, Hamtramck Township made a grant to a group of men, including George Hendrie and Emil Stroh. This grant was for a line to be built out Gratiot Avenue from a connection with Detroit City Railway's Gratiot line to Leesville, a town near Harper. The line was to be double tracked and the fare was to be a nickel. Service began on May 25, 1891, over a mile and one-half line and soon the official company name was Gratiot Avenue Railway. Detroit Suburban took over the line on November 1, 1892.

NORTH DETROIT AND CHENE RAILWAY (1891-1892)

On January 29, 1891, Hamtramck Township granted a franchise to William Livingston, George Russell and Thomas Baskerville, to operate a line from Bacon (Seven Mile) Road and Center Line Road (Van Dyke) to Chene Street and the Detroit City Limits, a distance of 5¼ miles. North Detroit had been originally called Norris, after the developer. The fare was to be seven cents for the first three years, and five cents thereafter.

In 1892, Baskerville transferred his interests to the other partners. Then on November 1, 1892, Detroit Suburban Railway acquired the franchise; then had Detroit Citizen Railway finish building the line. Service was provided by a single Healy motor. In July, 1895, the line was abandoned and the tracks removed, when according to the newspapers the line was failing to make money. Probably the cost to convert to an electric line would not have been worth the additional investment.

THE OTHER SUBURBAN OPERATIONS

The Detroit Suburban Railway Company consolidated most of the early street railway lines outside of the old city limits. One company, Detroit, Rouge River and Dearborn Railway, was left out of this group because of its location. Two other street railway lines in the northern part of the city were formed much later by promoters unrelated to the city lines.

DETROIT ROUGE RIVER AND DEARBORN RAILWAY (1889-1893)

Real estate promotions again served as the nucleus for the development of Detroit's fourth electric line. This time the developers including Strathern Hendrie, as company secretary, were at work on the far southwest portion of the city.

A company was incorporated on June 14, 1889, to operate a three-quarter mile of electric track from Woodmere Cemetery, at Dearborn Avenue, where it would connect with Fort Wayne and Belle Isle Railway, westward across the Rouge River on Fort Street. An interesting feature of the Springwells Township grant was a stipulation that "the quality of construction and equipment was to be equal to that of the Euclid Avenue line in Cleveland, Ohio". By August 14, 1889, work was progressing on track laying. Also, a boiler and engine was installed in a former fire house on the west bank of the Rouge River for power generation.

In the Street Railway Journal of January, 1892, it was reported that the company was running one car. Fort Wayne and Belle Isle Railway purchased the line by June, 1893, and operated it as a part of their route.

Mr. Lester E. Wise, former treasurer of the Detroit Rouge River and Dearborn Railway, many years later wrote an account of the line. Some excerpts from his memoirs are recorded here:

"In 1889, our organization opened a new subdivision out West Fort Street, west of the River Rouge. In those days only horsecars were used within Detroit. The Fort Wayne and Belle Isle Street Railway operated cars drawn by two horses on West Fort Street as far as Clark Street, and cars drawn by one horse from there to the entrance to Woodmere Cemetery. No cars ran west of Woodmere. The property this firm subdivided was three-quarters of a mile beyond the horsecar line, so the question of transportation was an important one. We decided to build and operate an electric street railway line from Woodmere on Fort Street, across the River Rouge through the property being subdivided, which was named Oakwood. The railway was organized and put into operation in the fall of 1889 and ran successfully by us for about two years. Our line became a part of the Fort Street Company which was taken over by the Citizens Street Railway and still later, merged into the D.U.R. Today, the road we built is a part of the Fort Street line now owned by the D.S.R.

Our troubles were many and varied. Fort Street at the time was not paved and most of the year a very bad road to travel. The rails we laid were of the old flat iron type, and the farmers who came to Detroit over Fort Street soon discovered that the streetcar tracks made a good wagon road. As a result, we were obliged to instruct the motormen, after giving fair warning to the farmer who refused to turn off the tracks when a car approached, to bump them. In one or two cases he carried out our instructions so well that farmers wagons were turned over into the ditch. It did not take very long to educate the farmers that the streetcar had the right-of-way, in fact they finally understood it better than some automobile drivers do today. Except for the facts above mentioned, in all the time we operated this line, no one was injured and no accidents occurred either with the car or at the power house. This, I believe is the best record of any streetcar line in the country if not the world. We had no strikes or labor troubles, it was also the cheapest transportation in the country, as fare was $.01 each way. A fare box was placed in the front end of the cars, and passengers deposited their fares in the box. As there was no conductor, passengers could "pay as you enter" or "pay as you leave", and everyone had a seat in the "GOOD OLD DAYS".

The three following illustrations were selected from a booklet, published in 1891, by the promoters of a land development project. The promoters also built the street railway so purchases could reach their new property. **ABOVE:** Crossing the Rouge River at Fort Street looking west. The first of three bridges to carry trolleys across the Rouge River at this point. **BELOW:** Looking east from end of line near Sanders. **Schramm Collection.**

THE DETROIT, UTICA AND ROMEO RAILWAY COMPANIES (1898-1901)

By the late 1890's many investors and promoters were eager to develop new territory. Many communities on the outlying areas of Detroit were equally as eager to have streetcar service. Such was the case with the Detroit, Utica and Romeo Railway and its promoter George E. Davis, State Representative. Davis proposed a thirty mile line north from Detroit via Van Dyke Road to Utica and Romeo. The company was incorporated on August 10, 1898, and franchises were quickly acquired through the various townships and villages the line would pass.

Approved motive power included the Kenetic System of stored steam, Patten Independent Electric Motor System, and the Trolley Electric Motor System. Hamtramck Township granted a franchise on October 7, 1898, for the company to lay track on Harper Avenue from the end of the electric railway to Van Dyke, then northward to the countyline. Then the Village of Warren issued a grant for the construction of a line from the northern to the southern town limits on Main Street, Railroad Street and Davy Street to the east city limits. The grant was amended in March, 1900, to extend the track to the northern limits of Warren township.

Davis's associates included Elliott G. Stevenson, one time mayor of Port Huron, and later legal counsel to various trolley projects around the State of Michigan. Yet capital was difficult to raise which caused construction to progress at a very slow rate. The road was reported operating one leased car by July 1, 1900, as far as the St. Clements Roman Catholic Church in Centerline, located two blocks north of Ten Mile Road, which was six and one quarter miles from its connection with the Detroit Electric Railway, at Harper.

The best thing going for the company was its franchise to Romeo and beyond to Imlay City. When the Detroit, Rochester and Romeo Railway planned a merger with the D.U.R. the Utica line with its franchises was absorbed with little cash trading hands. On September 4, 1901 the Detroit and Flint Railway was organized to bring all the fragments of remaining trolley lines under the control of D.U.R.

Just prior to the purchase of the Utica branch, Detroit United Railway's president, Jere Hutchins, assigned crews to inspect the lines to be acquired. The report dated July 15, 1901, estimated the earnings on both the Utica line and the new North Detroit line at $15,000. It would cost $2,000 for additional feeder line for the two systems, and $2,000 for track upgrading. On August 8, 1901, the line passed into the hands of the Detroit United Railway. The line to the Centerline Church was considered an interurban, but usually a city car serviced the line. It was later sold to the D.S.R. and became part of the Harper line. On January 23, 1899, Hamtramck Township issued a grant to Messers Simons and Winter of the Detroit, Rochester and Romeo Railway, and in late July was conveyed to the North Detroit Electric Railway. Trackage was proposed along Harper, St. Charles, Strong and Centerline (Van Dyke) to the township limits. A second route that was constructed, ran from the Michigan Central Railroad Crossing on Joseph Campau Avenue to Davison, to Mt. Elliott, to Nevada

(North Detroit). Much of this line was along the original line of the former North Detroit and Chene Railway, which had been torn up in 1895.

The Utica, Michigan, newspaper reported on December 22, 1900, that trolley service was available to Michigan Central Depot if passengers changed to a city car. The trolley fare was ten cents with two cars servicing the line. An advertisement of this type continued to run in the Utica paper for many months.

By summer 1901, the road was forced to sell to the Detroit United Railway. The Everett-Moore syndicate put pressure on the owners to sell out their holdings which included franchises to Flint. The sale took place on July 27, 1901, but a supplemental agreement dated August 8, 1901, called for the establishment of a transfer company called the Detroit and Flint Railway. It was incorporated August 10, 1901, and on October 10, 1901 this holding company took charge of the North Detroit line. This line in later years became part of the Baker then the Northwest Belt, and finally the Baker line again until it was abandoned.

The Citizens Company under R.T. Wilson did not desire to develop and operate too far beyond the city limits; thereby he left interurban operations between the larger cities for others. Accordingly, the major roads radiating from Detroit each had their own company providing service. But, as the interurbans reached the city limits the Citizens's crews took over their operation. It was not until the D.U.R. combined all the city operations that the surrounding interurban network was brought into one unified system. **BELOW:** An interurban of the Detroit and Pontiac Railway in downtown Detroit in 1897. This company was formed by a group which included George Hendrie who had operated the Detroit City Railway for many years. **Burton Historical Collection Detroit Public Library.**

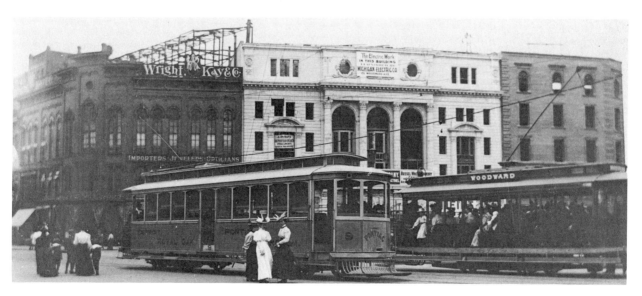

RIDING LINES - 1894

When first developed, street railway transportation was welcomed by the citizenry. But as time passed this love affair cooled. Newspapers tended to take journalistic jabs at the neglected streetcar system. A selection of these articles follow:

CASS AND THIRD

The service on the Cass and Third line for several years past has been so rocky that when the persons start down to business in the morning they invariably bid their family an affectionate farewell, knowing that the chances for their return before they are bowed and crippled with age are about even. Owing to the preponderance of time wasted by otherwise fond husbands on streetcars, Piety Hill is heavily stocked with Enoch Ardens. The wives are as faithful as the average, but their husbands are hung up so long between their homes and their business that they finally give them up for dead and marry again. The horses on the line are of peculiar brand. They were all born tired, if one of these should ever break out in a trot, the passengers would drop dead. The drivers are just the same. They are all gentlemen of elegant leisure. Their principal occupation, when not asleep is whistling. If there is any song or dance or comic opera that these quiet, unassuming gentlemen can't whistle, the patrons are unacquainted with it.

In making a summary of the numberless excellencies of this great street railway line, the tracks must not be forgotten. They are full of frogs and toads and other reptiles which have been added to the repertory for the sole purpose of throwing the car off the tracks. They are a howling success. One of the most familiar and soul stirring spectacles connected with the entire layout is presented by the passengers picking the disabled cars out of the gutters at frequent intervals and replacing them upon the strap rails with all the tenderness and respect due advanced age. Every business man who has patronized the line for any considerable length of time wears callouses on his hands as big as English Walnuts. He has no choice in the matter. If he doesn't help to lug the car back to its legitimate moorings, the driver will strike up a new tune and head for the barn to get a fresh start. As he uses the paving instead of the tracks, for the return journey, the number of times the digestive organs of the passengers are turned over during the trip can be readily figured out.

It is scarcely worth while to allude to the fact that the cars are packed like sardine boxes. Where a lifetime is consumed in making a round trip, it is only natural that they should pick up a many good people. A business man who dies of old age is very apt to want to die at home, whenever possible. In order to accomplish this on The Cass and Third Line, he has to get up very early and keep going.

At Third (Hamilton) and Holden in 1890, a turntable was used to reverse direction of the horsecars. On the running board of car 134 is Will Woodruff. **Burton Historical Collection Detroit Public Library.**

MICHIGAN LINE

There is not a straight rail on the four streaks of scrap iron on that great avenue between the Campus and Trumbull and the wretched cobblestone pavement is all out of shape between the rails and the space between the rails and the space between the double tracks, which is also a patch work of cobble and limestone chips.

Every possible crook and twist is in the rails, vertical and horizontal, and nearly all of them are dished inwards. The wonder on casting the eye along such tracks is how the cars are kept on them at all, but is explained when you ride, they go so slow that they take the curvatures, and more than half the time they remain on the tracks. But they are off frequently and often run three and four blocks before they are righted again. There is no appliance for putting them back on the tracks except such as the conductor can pick up in the street in the way of a stone or a stick to guide the car back, and passengers rattle their bones over the stones and hang on for dear life as the car surges and bangs along after the desperately strained horses. The change from the comfortively smooth line on Trumbull to that of Michigan is like that from a landlocked harbor to rough open water. Morning and evening the traffic is the heaviest, but it doesn't seem to make any difference in the arrangements. Cars run at the same intervals so far as the laymen can judge, and daily as the crowd offers it is stuffed into the car as it comes along at the same old jog, and the voice of the conductor is heard, "move along up there", "there's room in this seat, five in a seat".

Five in a seat is the rule (open cars) when the crowd is to be stuffed in and yet a seat will hold but four average sized persons with any comfort and five large sized persons will actually be squeezed together. But it is a question of rule and not of judgement with the conductor. Seven women have been counted in one seat. On the open cars the conductors have a habit. They collect fares by reaching over the outside rail and they explain that if they collected from the inside rail that they would be struck by passing cars on the other track, the cars come so close together in passing. The peculiar habit alluded to lies in frequent necessity the conductor has for lying across a ladies lap when he stretches himself for a distant fare. And if the distant gentleman on the far side does not lean over the strange lady at his side to meet the conductor half way he gets a piece of the conductors mind for not complying with the rules of the company.

Before the days of the electric streetcar in Detroit, the horse car served the main streets of the city. This relaxing scene took place a short distance from the center of town on the Michigan Line at Third Street. **Burton Historical Collection Detroit Public Library.**

Sometime after 1885 the horse car struck a pose for the camera. Originally heat was not provided the passenger, but by this date a law demanded heaters in each car. Note the stove pipe protruding above the car roof. **D.S.R. Files.**

RIDING LINES - 1894

CONGRESS AND BAKER

The Congress and Baker line begins at Woodward and Congress and ends near the sunset at the intersection of Livernois and Dix after penetrating the weedy regions of Daniel Scottens vacant lots, where little frame churches, corner groceries and pretty little children abound. It isn't such a very bad streak of old iron. Cars don't plunge as frantically here as they do on the Mack Avenue or the Leesville extension. They only give a succession of rocking horse kicks between curves themselves like a cow in a cotillion.

It is a little bit exciting at the Michigan Central Bridge on Baker (Bagley), and rather enjoyable for the contrast between the monotonous trot, trot of the team and the plunge up the steep side of the bridge. At the bridge they do the Ben-Hur act with three horses and the sleepy old car is changed for a minute into a fiery and inspiring chariot flying upward as all fiery chariots do. The third horse to assist up the bridge is a stocky little roan that enters into the spirit of the plunge, chews his bits and spits foam and lays his ears back and twitches his tail as he is hooked on. Then whoop, up, up she goes and over the bridge she is. And then she strikes the same gait, hump, slew, stagger, jolt, jar, bang, bump keeping monotonous time with the putter, putter, clink, clink, clank, of the shoes of the horses on the cobblestone pavement.

GRATIOT

The Gratiot Avenue streetcar line is a horse car line. Rope harnesses, straw collars and all of the appliances discarded with Noah's Ark as a means of transportation. It's rapid transit only when the driver uses the whip a cut which isn't often. Gratiot Avenue line is like the description of the western road that began in a broad avenue, ran into a single track turnpike, thence into a cow path and then into a squirrel track and ran up a tree. Gratiot extends from broad and smooth Woodward Avenue, pursues the ample breadth of Monroe Avenue crooks around into Randolph Street, enters Gratiot Avenue, wiggles into the Leesville extension and disappears. They have got a good heavy girder rail flush with the

In 1885 the Gratiot line operated 1¾ miles from downtown to the Grand Trunk Railroad crossing. In the background at the left was the railroad station. **D. Moore Collection.**

pavement and in fair business shape as far as the Detroit, Grand Haven and Milwaukee railway crossing over which the "hoss" car rolls along like a respectable funeral. At that point the old strap rail and trouble begins. Here between the stone pavement lies the double tracks in a gutter about a foot and one half below the grade of the street. It would prove to be a puzzle to a stranger as to why tracks should run in such poor shape. In the rainy season there are some elegant puddles for ducks along this stretch of the Gratiot Avenue line to Mc Dougal where the wood paving begins. Here the line looms up flush to grade again and there is a change from the flanged cobblestone center to wood pavement between the tracks that matches the rest of the street. If it were not for the blessing of light traffic, this stretch of the road even to the terminus at Sheridan Avenue would be a scrap heap by the end of the season. The Leesville extension of the Gratiot Avenue line is a single track, Bob Tail (but with two men per bob), plug line, that is something on the side as it runs near the ditch when it runs at all and doesn't rear up and throw a car. Anyone that has had occasion to go to the Schuteenfest knows the Leesville extension and shutters at the knowledge. Leesville extension Bob Tail cars don't run, they prance. It is like riding an ill trained saddle horse or a lame dromedary, your entire attention is devoted to keeping inside the car. Of course it is not just the instinct of a bob tailed car to jump up and kick, all that is due to the rails and pulling powers of the horse. All trains on this road are wild trains. Dogs along the road do not run outside the fence to bark at the bob-tail as experience has taught then that the

car is apt to suddenly leave the track and take the skin off a dog. There is a church up the line where, as reports go, the prayers of the congregation are offered for the safe return of members who intend to take a trip downtown. Yet the Leesville Bob-tail isn't the worst road in Detroit.

MACK AVENUE

A ride over the Mack Avenue line and its extension to Grosse Pointe will cure dyspepsia, if violent exercise is a specific for that disease. Starting in at Elmwood, on a car with faded paint which resembles a picture of discomfort, your gaze is attracted to the line and road bed on ahead. The lines of rails looking like a pair of elongated streaks of rust seemingly in a state of active wriggling, like a pair of long and badly attenuated garter snakes, as though desirous of escaping from the futile labor of trying to hold a car on the tracks.

The rails are old fashioned straps, crooked dished, humped and depressed as though the hard times and the pounding of the few cars had taken the life out of them and they wanted to get out of the street railway business. The city is paving a long stretch of Mack out from Elmwood; but this doesn't seem to make any difference with the rails of the road, as they seem badly demoralized along the new pavement as they are elsewhere, if not worse, since the motorman appeared to feel more assured of the situation on the unpaved line than he was on the paved.

A motorman can not have any eye flirtations with the young ladies along the line of the Mack Avenue road, such as he does on the heavier railed Jefferson line. A Mack Avenue motorman glues his eyes to the irregularly wriggled span of rails ahead of him, ready to shut off and throw his whole soul into the brakes at the frequent ugly spots where the bouncing car would be sure to be ditched were she allowed to go at the tremendous speed of seven miles per hour, which she accomplishes on the good spots. But doesn't detect the bad spots all the time and as a consequence the passengers are alternately bouncing and setting down hard and trying to look unconcerned. No conversation is indulged in, as all of the passengers are too deeply interested in the energetic efforts of the motorman to plug her at the right spot, and to give the devil his due. The motorman does avoid some of the worst spots by bringing the car up with a jerk to nearly a standstill. Looking out of the car, the landscape appears to be terraces under the violent up and down motion of the car. At St. Clair Heights you get out and wait for the car on the Grosse Pointe extension and take a needed rest.

When the connecting car is in motion, undreamed of troubles begin. You are off strap rail and on light T rail and you settle down to comfort, but sit in misery. What with short curves and a track that has seen the service of a lifting gang since mankind ate the first apple, what you have left is happiness compared with misery. The car actually took such mad plunges into the ruts that infest this infernal road that the trolley was thrown off the wires twice in half a mile. Passengers were tossed again at each other and if the plunge happened to be taken on a short curve the up coming bump threw the passengers up and gave them a half twist at the same time. It was enough to make a persons hair raise with horror when the car dove at Conner's Creek Bridge and made a noise exactly similar to that of several tons of scrap iron thrown from a height to a brick sidewalk.

The bridge is good enough, but the car has a fearfully complicated way of crossing it. The central portions of passengers are badly fatigued when they reach Grosse Pointe. At Grosse Pointe the people said that the road hadn't been touched since it was first built, and that every car cut its own grass. Down at St. Clair Heights the groceryman accounted for the condition of the road by venturing the opinion that the owners were dead and that the heirs were fighting for it in the courts. If both sections of this extremely interesting iron way, with its snorting, cavorting and fiery car, were sold for old iron, the proceeds might keep the heirs out of the poorhouse for a week. (And so ended the horsecar era.)

There are no known photos of the early Mack electrics; therefore, we included this shot of 299 in service on Woodward during 1893-1895. Note the open front platform on this Pullman built car which shares the street with horse car 38 of the Chene line. **Burton Historical Collection Detroit Public Library.**

Chapter 3—The Detroit United Railway

FORMATION OF THE D.U.R

It was past midnight when there came a knock on the New York Astor Hotel room door of Tom Johnson. Upon answering the raps of the unexpected caller, Tom discovered Richard Thornton (R.T.) Wilson at the door. Wilson, a wealthy investment broker in New York, had been working closely with Tom Johnson in his Detroit and Brooklyn streetcar investments. But, now, he explained his early morning visit was the result of building frustrations which had driven him to wander the streets at night. He discussed with Tom Johnson how the business world was creating within him a contempt for life around him. Wilson had grown up in Georgia enjoying the peaceful country life. Then the Civil War threw him into many unexpected occupations of which one sent him to Europe to represent the Confederate Army in selling cotton. It was the result of this experience that brought him to New York City in 1867 and the world of finance. He stated he had tried to get out of the world of finance but that only brought on a meloncholy mood. So into the early hours of the morning the two talked.

Tom Johnson was emotionally moved by this man. After days of soul searching, Tom came to the conclusion he would never end up like that. To this end he planned to sell out his streetcar companies in Detroit and Brooklyn, plus his steel mills.

The result of this change of life style was the search for a buyer for his streetcar system. There just so happened to be two men in Cleveland who were buying every streetcar line they could find for sale in the Great Lakes area. One of these partners in the expanding syndicate was part owner in a few of the Johnson-Wilson Detroit streetcar companies, The Detroit Electric Railway and the Fort Wayne and Belle Isle Railway. Johnson and Wilson met with this group known as the Everett-Moore Syndicate to work out details of the sale. The financial transaction took months to settle.

R.T. Wilson up to his old tricks of fast dealing, was trying to short change Tom Johnson. Therefore in late December, 1900, Johnson took Wilson to court to get his fair share of the new organization. Tom Johnson considered himself 1/5 owner of the Citizens and any side deal made by Wilson and Everette would not be settled by Johnson's interest being negated. By December 30, Johnson and Wilson had resolved their differences.

Jere Hutchins, then Vice-Presedent of the Citizens, shuttled back and forth between Detroit and New York City as he worked to evaluate the system so a settlement could be reached. At the final meeting of the sale, just prior to the December 31, 1900, take over date of the new company, a new name was discussed. In later years, Hutchins recalled the incident the following way; !

"A group of stockholders forming the new company sat in the office of R.T. Wilson in New York City. After the basis of the new company was settled an unnamed stockholder asked,

"And by what name shall the new babe be called"? A Detroit voice was raised, "How would Detroit United Railway do"? "Excellent", replied the group in chorus".

The D.U.R. as the company became known was formed on the following basis:

The Detroit Citizens Railway received the largest share in the stock exchange, 65% or 81,043 shares out of the 125,000 shares offered. The Detroit Suburban Railway was offered one dollar because by this time all property was under control of the Detroit Citizens Street Railway. Of the two remaining lines - The Detroit, Fort Wayne and Belle Isle Railway received 22% and The Detroit Electric Railway received 13% of the shares. The new company assumed the indebtedness of all the absorbed companies.

It took E.W. Moore and H. Everett two months longer to arrange the purchase of R.T. Wilson's interests in the D.U.R. In a sense the Detroit property was back under the management of the builders of Mayor Pingree's, Three cent lines.

Now in firm control of the new company that comprised all the Detroit City lines, the Everett-Moore Syndicate, holders of many telephone and transit systems in the Great Lakes area, set forth a policy of a massive expansion program. Here-to-fore the previous owner believed in only a city transit system. But Mr. Everett stated that he firmly believed that in another decade there would be practically one solid city from Port Huron to Buffalo. His syndicate intended to control all of it. To help finance the expansion program, the syndicate tried to sell D.U.R. stock in Detroit at $70.00 per share which was $8.00 below the Cleveland price. Even at this bargain price Detroiters did not rush to purchase the D.U.R. stock. It was eventually sold to Canadian interests.

By February 15, 1901, the syndicate had firm control of the Detroit United Railway. They quickly set about the purchase of the independent trolley lines entering the city. Within six months, five companies had come under control of the D.U.R.

Date	D.U.R. Division	Detroit Street	Miles of Trackage	Former Company Name
2-20-01	Wyandotte	West Fort	10.980	Wyandotte & Detroit River
5-1-01	Orchard Lake	Grand River	58.770	Detroit & Northwestern
6-1-01	Pontiac	Woodward	36.522	Detroit & Pontiac
8-1-01	Flint	Center Line Chene Street	85.307	Detroit, Rochester Romeo & Lake Orion
8-31-01	Windsor	Located across the Detroit River in Canada		Sandwich, Windsor & Amherstberg Railway

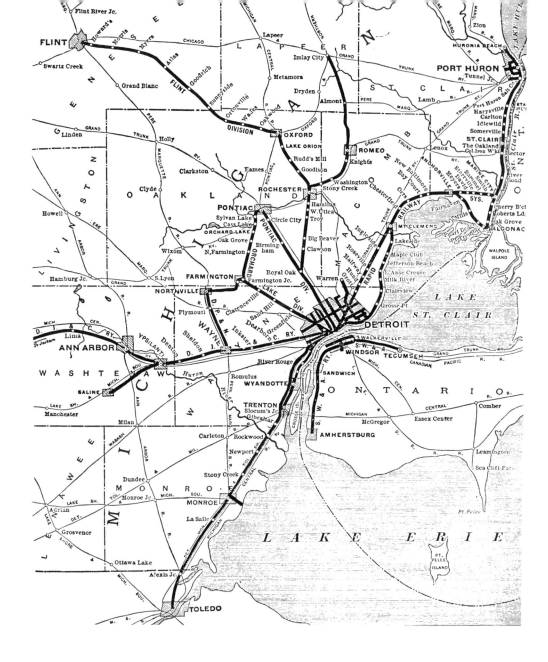

Control of the stock of the Rapid Railway System was acquired in October of 1901, by the D.U.R. Now all major routes into Detroit were controlled by the D.U.R., except Michigan Avenue. This route was controlled by the Hawks-Angus Syndicate which operated the Detroit, Ypsilanti, and Ann Arbor Railway. It was not until 1907 that this line came under the control of the D.U.R. Other interurban lines were being added in 1901. The Everett-Moore Syndicate considered a new bond issue to obtain money to purchase the Ann Arbor line for further expansion, however the conditions of the city franchises which in some cases were to expire in 6 to 9 years made this impractical. The company did not want to request a new franchise due to sentiment favoring a three cent fare as existing franchises allowed a five cent fare on the best paying lines. The Everett-Moore Syndicate had other priorities. One was the connection of their Lake Shore System from Cleveland to Toledo to Detroit. This was the construction of the Detroit and Toledo Short Line; a high speed line connecting Toledo with Detroit.

In total, they had 1500 miles under their control or in construction during the year 1901. It was too much. They had over extended their available funds and the banks called their notes on February 5, 1902 forcing the syndicate into bankruptcy. The Detroit & Toledo Short Line was a casualty of the fallen holding company. It was sold to a group of railroads including the Grand Trunk Railroad, and is presently operated as the Detroit and Toledo Shore Line Railroad. The D.U.R. was not directly involved as only the D.U.R. stock still held by the Everett-Moore Syndicate was involved in the bankruptcy. These shares were purchased by additional Canadian interests. In later years the Canadian interests totally controlled the D.U.R. But for the present, the D.U.R. continued to operate as a well managed corporation with Jere Hutchins as the newly elected President replacing Everett. Traffic increased as improvements were completed. The Toledo connection was reopened in 1904. Through the years portions of the interurban lines became integrated into the city system.

"WHY THE TROLLEY!"

ABOVE: Gratiot and City Limits (Harper) May 9, 1908. The Rapid Railway track was on the right.

ABOVE: Showing the three tracks on Woodward north of Jefferson with an interurban using the middle track.
BELOW: A northbound interurban at Woodward and Grand River. **Schramm Collection.**

ABOVE: Pontiac bound interurban 7539 passing Soldiers and Sailors Monument in September, 1916. Note the similarity with the city cars as the D.U.R. tried to keep as low a profile in the city as possible. **BELOW:** Griswold Street had its daily crush of people and streetcars as evidenced in this August 1921 photo. Interurban 7110 is bound for Farmington. **Manning Brothers Historical Collection.**

ABOVE: Taken August 1914, this photo shows Rapid Railway car 7293 heading out Monroe Avenue for Port Huron. **BELOW:** An interurban has just turned the corner off Michigan onto Griswold in this October 1920 shot. **Manning Brothers Historical Collection.**

THE D.U.R. vs CITY HALL

"A city transit system that is privately owned usually is placed in an untenable position in that it must give satisfactory service and make suffcient money to cover debts and cost of operation. A transit company is one industry open to public concern so that much tact must be used concerning fares, equipment, free transfers and services," so stated Tom Johnson, before leaving for Cleveland.

The aspiring politicians and those in office usually looked for an issue that could create emotional reaction and Ex-Mayor Pingree had given Detroiters two; the three cent fare, and free universal transfers. After rising to the Governership on such issues, he added another; municipal ownership. The next 22 year period in Detroit saw very little expansion of lines. Rather it became a time when politicians took verbal pot shots at the D.U.R.'s fares, equipment, and services.

After formation of the D.U.R., trackage was relatively static for several years until 1909 when the first large amount of the trackage franchises expired. During the years the franchises were to expire as follows;

Date	Track Miles	Date	Track Miles
1906	3.23	1919	1.14
1909	52.39	1921	13.90
1910	15.64	1924	54.59
1915	3.05	1927	1.23
1916	15.55	1928	3.08
1917	1.27	1935	4.85

Accordingly, no move to make any fare agreements were attempted until 1906. The fare at this time was a straight five cents except on the "Pingree three cent lines" as everyone called then.

The city government was still considering municipal ownership and in 1905 appropriated ten thousand dollars to construct lines to be leased to an operating company. An injunction was issued and the case went up as far as the State Supreme Court which ruled the appropriation illegal.

In 1906, after long discussions, the City Council had the Codd-Hutchins amendment placed on the fall ballot. The amendment was supported by the incumbent Mayor, George P. Codd, but William Thompson the opposition candidate opposed it. Among the items voted on was a lower fare; ten tickets for $.25 in place of the eight for $.25 Workingman's tickets then in use. These new tickets were to be called Industrial Tickets. In addition they would be good for an additional hour each day. The balance of the day the fare would return to the six tickets for $.25, and there would be universal transfers. The D.U.R. agreed to maintain the roadway twelve inches out from the track. In return, the D.U.R. wanted all franchises to end December 24, 1924, the date the old Detroit Railway franchises

expired. Mayor Codd and the proposition he backed, both were defeated.

The Detroit News was a major agitator for the defeat of the proposal. They wrote editorials and published cartoons, which influenced the public attitude toward the amendment. Even Tom Johnson, now the Mayor of Cleveland, came to Detroit and offered to build a three cent line. He would build lines in areas not having service and take over the expired D.U.R. franchises, with the knowledge that in a few years franchises would expire on the best lines such as Fort and Woodward. But, the city officials declined the offer on grounds that only municipal ownership would be acceptable.

Again, the city officials tried another approach this time, in 1907, passing an ordinance called the Halley Ordinance. The ordinance required a fare of five tickets for $.15 on all lines where the entire line or a portion of its franchise had expired. This was appealed through the Federal Courts by the Guaranty Title & Trust Company of New York owners of $25,000,000 of D.U.R. bonds. Then Judge Swan ruled the Halley Ordinance illegal.

Then on September 17, 1907, a proposal was placed on the ballot which would allow extensions of much needed lines allowing both the three cent and five cent fares depending on which line was extended. Naturally, the Mayor and Detroit News opposed it. They wanted a three cent fare across the board and the proposal failed.

In 1909 the City established the "Committee of Fifty", to study the transit needs, to put a valuation on the system, and to review the fare structure. The Committee reported that there was a need for 58 miles of new double track and 26 miles of single track that should be converted to double. Also, re-routings were needed in the downtown area to relieve traffic congestion. Another recommendation they felt imperative was to form the nucleus of a subway to contribute to the rapid growth and developement of the city. The subway should be built by the City and leased to the street car company until the City takeover. The increase in the number of passengers in 1908 over 1898 was as follows:

Passengers

	Revenue	Transfer	Total
1908	107,393,502	40,447,333	148,840,835
1898	44,197,122	11,181,796	55,378,918

As fifty-two miles of track franchises expired, the D.U.R. agreed to pay a daily rental of three hundred dollars to continue to use their own tracks. This November 13, 1909 agreement was only a stop gap measure until the franchise problems could be settled on the trackage that was covered by the franchise which expired on November 14th.

The Committee of Fifty resigned in 1910 due to failure to arrive at any agreement on valuation. Mr. Barcroft, appraiser for the city, had placed a value on the traction companies property of $11,284,579. While

Mr. Rifenback, D.U.R.'s appraiser had placed the valuation at $24,708,342 exclusive of goodwill or franchises. This disagreement as to the market value of the property stalemated the sale of the streetcar company for many years.

The D.U.R. felt the voters in Detroit did not want municipal ownership, yet they could not obtain the additional franchises or extensions of old ones. But Detroit was still doubling its population every ten years. Therefore, the D.U.R. decided to enter into a track extension program of eight miles on what was to be called "Day to Day" agreements. There was to be no franchise and the city would be able to purchase the track at any time, the price to be fixed by a three party arbitration panel. The trackage to be built was on Hamilton from Holden to the city limits and a track on Grandy from North Chene (Joseph Campau) to Gratiot, and to double track Mack Avenue. This agreement was reached on April 4, 1911. Under this type of agreement, all D.U.R. city trackage was built until the city take over.

TOP: This often seen photograph of a crowded 600 series open bench car was used to describe the conditions of Detroit's streetcars. It may have been posed or taken at the change of shifts. **CENTER:** Car 534 crossing Woodward; in the background is car 550. Note the absence of automobiles. **BOTTOM:** A 1902 view of Woodward north of Jefferson showing a good mixture of cars. Visible is an open bench car; a single trucker pulling a work trailer; a Rapid Railway interurban; and a Pontiac interurban. **D.S.R. Files.**

On April 9,1911, a few days later, the city decided to raise the track rental from three hundred dollars to five hundred dollars per day. This was based on the addition of the expired franchise on the Fort Street line. The City Attorney stated in court briefs that the company was an outlaw on the streets. The company noted that of the 16 miles involved on Fort Street, 10 miles of track were laid in brick and the company engineers estimated that it would take 161 days to remove the track, without allowing time to replace the pavement. General Manager Brooks stated that the affected tracks serviced both the main shops where most repairs were made to the 1100 to 1200 city cars, and the Clark Car House.

Depending on whose side you supported, the year 1912 was both good and bad for the traction factions. A fare ordinance was submitted to the voters, and again defeated because of agitation for city ownership. Then the State Supreme Court ruled the rental charges illegal. However, the city could order the streets vacated. This ruling was to be a most important weapon in forcing the D.U.R. from the streets in later years.

In 1913, the voters approved the Charter Amendment providing for municipal ownership and operations within ten miles of the city. On July 29th, under this act, the first Detroit Street Railway Commission was appointed. It's members were:

John Dodge	Partner, Dodge Brothers Motor Car Co.
James Couzens	General Manager, Ford Motor Company
William Mahon	Vice-President of the American Federation of Labor.

Mr. Mahon resigned in 1914 and was replaced by Mr. James Wilkie, superintendent of the mechanical department of Parke, Davis and Company. Throughout the years the D.S.R. Commission often included automotive company executives. In one dispute with the D.U.R. over fares and service these Commissioners threatened to put 1000 automobiles on the streets if the D.U.R. failed to provide the service. The D.U.R. was forced to absorb a wage increase with no fare increase on this occasion. No conflict of interest inquiries were made into this situation throughout the years. Today, Detroit does not have a rapid transit system while urban areas of less population have a system.

In 1913, the City attempted to operate a coach line on Junction Street after refusing the D.U.R.'s request to build a streetcar line. They even borrowed D.U.R. fare registers for their own use, installed them on buses which the city (Department of Parks and Boulevards) used to operate over the Belle Isle Bridge. The fare was three cents and after a short time of losing money, the city cancelled the operation.

On August 5, 1913, Jere Hutchins made a proposal of seven tickets for $.25 good for twenty-four hours. The fares on the Pingree three cent lines and the Workingmans tickets, to remain the same. He also agreed to pay $75,000 to the city for operating privileges in lieu of the rental which had not been paid since July 24, 1910. On August 7th, the City Council approved the proposal and the new fare became effective.

A report of Detroit's transit needs begun in 1914 by Barclay, Parsons & Klapp was submitted to the D.S.R. Commissioners the following year. It again recommended a subway and the re-routing of several lines to relieve congestion in the downtown area and the use of larger cars (3000 series type) and the large trailers (5000 series). The D.U.R. purchased the larger cars and trailers and re-routed several lines. However, the subway proposal was talked about, but there was no further action.

Again the city was attempting to purchase the D.U.R. and made an offer of $24,900,00, on February 23, 1915. The D.U.R. Directors and Stockholders accepted the offer on March 31, 1915. This offer was withdrawn after the newspapers made a fuss, so the

A view of Griswold Street looking north from the rear of City Hall. The early vintage autos at the right are most interesting. **D.S.R. Files.**

Long lines awaiting service in Campus Martius 1920. Building a rapid transit system, instead of insisting on more streetcars on the already crowded streets may have been a better solution. **Manning Brothers Historical Collection.**

J. C. HUTCHINS
DETROIT
PRESIDENT AND GENERAL MANAGER
DETROIT UNITED RAILWAY

D.S.R. Commission re-submitted a lower offer of $23,285,000. The D.U.R. refused the offer on April 29, 1915, and the battle continued. Many newspapers would be sold telling the public how the campaign to rid the city of the D.U.R. was progressing.

Then to settle the problem of the valuation the D.U.R. and city agreed to have the city take over the lines the following January 1st, and let a panel of Circuit Court Judges establish a fair price. The newspapers and other opposition labeled this "the-pig-in-a-poke-plan" and the voters defeated it.

In April 1919, another proposal to purchase the D.U.R. for $31,500,000 was rejected by the voters. After this defeat, Mayor James Couzens (former D.S.R. Commissioner), decided to build a competing system to force the D.U.R. off the streets. The following year in April, the voters approved funds to begin construction. Then on April 17, 1922, the voters approved purchase of the D.U.R., which resulted in the city take over of all single fare operations in Detroit on May 15, 1922.

The D.U.R. had been backed to the wall. Stockholders and Corporate Officers, mostly Montreal investors, bent under the pressure of "Big Jim" Couzens. They even went against the advice of their corporate leader Jere Hutchins to hold out for a better deal. The company accepted the offer of $19,850,000. The city prepared to accept responsibility to operate the then largest municipal street railway in the world.

James Couzens shortly would leave office to become U.S. Senator and Jere Hutchins retire to his Grosse Pointe home. The trolley system was now in the hands of City Hall, a management destined to retire the streetcar in favor of the bus. The operational change to buses began shortly after the city take over and was completed thirty-five years later, when the last trolley rolled into the Woodward Car House, April 8, 1956.

ABOVE: Downtown Detroit October 1916 prior to World War 1. **BELOW:** The motorman was forced to contend with narrow main streets and a mixture of vehicles. **Manning Brothers Historical Collection.**

Preceeding the 1906 election these two tickets appeared, one called the Industrial Ticket with a 10 for 25¢ fare good during working hours, was actually put into use on October 22, 1906. The other ticket calling for a 3¢ fare all hours was a political item put out by the opposition, which won the election. On November 6, 1906 the Industrial Tickets were withdrawn from use.

On April 7, 1919, the voters of Detroit were asked to approve the purchase of the D.U.R. properties for $31,500,000. This proposition was turned down. One reason attributed to the defeat was Henry Ford's "declaration that he would revolutionize transportation by building a light, gasoline-driven street car that would operate on rails and bear the same relation to present streetcars as the "Tin Lizzie" does to other automobiles." The American Railway Association review of the incident continued by quoting Mr. Sorenson, Ford's General Manger, "Is not a street car but is a interurban or steam road proposition, driven by two 80 hp engines, capable of making 70 miles per hour. "Mr. Sorenson went on to say this car was just an experiment and may not prove out at all. The article finished by noting the price of gasoline at ten times the cost of electricity, and the life of a gasoline motor one-quarter that of the average electric motor in streetcar service. On these two pages we have included photos and a letter written by Mr. Ford in reply to criticism to Mr. Sorenson's statements. **Material from the Schramm and Henning Collections.**

Henry Ford
Detroit

Apr
16th
1919

Mailed Received

APR 18 1919

Board of Street Railway Commissioners
Detroit
Michigan

Gentlemen:

Your letter of April 12th received this
morning at Dearborn after having been delivered to
the Ford Motor Company.

It is my belief that the Commission has
taken upon itself a great responsibility in assuming
that the recently submitted purchase plan was defeated
because of statements made by Mr Charles E Sorensen,
which would indicate that the people of the City of
Detroit are not capable of deciding matters of such
importance for themselves.

Repudiation by the voters of the street car
plan as submitted, which evidently represented the
best arrangement you felt capable of formulating,
makes it seem questionable in my mind whether or not
you can claim to represent the people of the City of
Detroit, and when you are able to furnish me with
reasonable assurance of this fact, I will be glad to
co-operate with you in working out the development of
a new type of gas or electric car for street railway
purposes.

However, the question of whether or not we
will co-operate with you, or any other accredited
representatives of the City of Detroit, will not deter
us in any way from carrying out what we have already
undertaken in such development, and when we are ready
to demonstrate the merits of the new type of street
car, it will be left for the judgment of the Citizens
of Detroit.

Very truly yours

Henry Ford

HF:Z

HENRY FORD

DEARBORN

TOP: Thirteen car lines converged upon the downtown area. The first lines constructed operated on the major streets. Later lines used the side streets. In this case the Fourteenth car line passed through the downtown area on Clifford - Griswold - Shelby - Jefferson - Woodbridge - Bates - Farmer - Gratiot - Broadway, and Witherell. Car 118 approaches Gratiot while on Broadway as it heads towards its Fourteenth terminal. **BELOW:** The Baker car line crew pose for the camera with their long switch tool in hand. It took a motorman well versed with the city to negotiate his car over and around the numerous hand throw switches on the circuitous car routes. **Both Schramm Collection.**

ABOVE: Campus Martius is located on the east side of Woodward across from the old City Hall. As this location was the meeting point of eight car lines it was usually the scene of intense activity as portrayed in this early 20th century photograph. **The Burton Historical Collection Detroit Public Library. BELOW:** Six car lines converged to share trackage in this area south of City Hall. **Manning Brothers Historical Collection.**

D.U.R. OPERATIONS

The Superintendent of operations had the responsibility of keeping the system moving whether it concerned the movement of cars, selling of tickets, track, or power. Mr. H.A. Stanley was the first person appointed to this post at the D.U.R. Jere Hutchins discovered this talented employee in the scheduling department and advanced him through the ranks until he was appointed Superintendent of Operations.

Stanley left the D.U.R. in 1903 to take charge of other systems, but his father remained in the employ of the D.U.R. until retirement. Stanley eventually was appointed head of London Transport, and by 1914 he was knighted Sir Albert Stanley, after World War I, he received the title of Lord Ashfield.

Under the control of the general superintendent H.A. Stanley, were six categories of responsibility; the power stations, repair shops, track, overhead, passenger agents and the dispatcher.

THE DIVISIONS

The D.U.R. divided the system into seven transportation divisions by 1902. Each unit superintendent had two or more lines under him, depending on the length of the lines and traffic conditions. Each of these Division Superintendents had at least one assistant. At each of the car houses were day and night foreman. The Division Superintendent had nothing to do with the rolling stock while in the car house other than to see it was kept clean. The motor inspections were under the motive power department.

Scheduling of cars for service was critical. On city streets, cars averaged 10.67 miles per hour over the 187 miles of track. The closest headway on the heavy lines was 30 seconds at 6 P.M. On the crosstown, main north and south lines this headway was maintained during the rush hours, which varied according to the franchises covering the line. Usually this rush hour period was from 5:30 a.m. to 8:00 a.m., and from 5:15 to 6;15 p.m., with 1804 runs scheduled. Many of the runs were less than 45 minutes, never the less the total system had only 1221 city cars available for service if 100% were in working order. As riders increased, the company did continue to purchase equipment. The 1919 Bemis Report listed 1434 passenger cars available for service.

Some lines issued transfers with tickets and some required an additional charge, even on a rush hour schedule. Owing to the fare being much lower at certain hours in the morning and evening rush hours there resulted an enormous congestion of traffic within these periods. The factories and institutions employing labor adopted their working hours to suit the period when the discounted tickets were good. As a result, the D.U.R. was required to increase its service during rush hours 139% above the base to serve these abnormal traffic surges within the rush periods.

CONDUCTORS AND MOTORMEN

Another responsibility of the Division Superintendents was the operating personnel. The conductors and motormen were hired by the company employ-ment bureau and in early days the turnover rate was 60%. An elaborate point, or merit system was adopted January 2, 1902, as a means of social justice. Out of this system came the famous expression, "Brownie Points". In the past, an employee would be suspended (laid off work without pay) for breaking a company rule. The result the D.U.R. felt was that the family suffered from the loss of pay. Therefore, the, "Brown Merit System" was adopted which, in place of only suspensions, the employee was allowed to continue working until there were enough points against him, then he would be discharged. Also, good practices or acts would earn the employee points. The company stated that after six months under the plan, 37 men were discharged, however, the slowdowns had been greatly reduced. In an article regarding this plan an example was given on how a car crew, to obtain additional points, had removed a wire to enable them to maintain their schedule instead of waiting for the repair crew. Through the years this plan was laid aside and replaced by a review board which has the power to discharge.

ROLLING STOCK

Repair of rolling stock was under the power department, according to the 1902 organization chart. The company had their major shops on Jefferson Avenue and Bellvue, presently the site of a U. S. Rubber Company facility. 1905, these shops had been replaced by the larger Monroe Shops located in an area bounded by Monroe, Macomb, Dequindere, and St. Aubin Streets. This plant originally was The Detroit Car and Manufacturing Company bought by George Pullman, and for many years the fabrication center of Pullman Cars, until the company moved to Chicago. Since 1893, the plant had laid idle, but in 1902, the D.U.R., realizing the need for more space, purchased and modified the plant to their needs. This remained the central shops until problems with the city began over trackage rights on streets servicing this property. Then in 1915, the D.U.R. built their large Highland Park property which removed their facility from any future Detroit threats. This property across from the original Ford Plant in Highland Park was north of a private right-of-way and extended west from Woodward to Hamilton Avenues. The D.U.R. built streetcars at all three of the central shops however, here at Highland Park the large city double truck cars and trailers were built. After the city take over, the remaining property was used by the D.U.R. to service the suburban cars and interurbans. Through the years the D.U.R., usually pruchased car bodies separate from the trucks and motors and installed them in their own shops.

A style of car developed in Detroit which became popular throughout the trolley world. This style was called the "Detroit platform". Most city cars had the extended rear platform which gave additional standing room. The platform was permanently enclosed on one side, with a wide opening on the side of agress and exit. The novel feature of the platform was an iron railing, which divided it into two portions and was designed to prevent passengers standing on the platform from interferring with the passengers entering or leaving the car. This platform had been developed by the Citizens Railway as one of their first items after taking over so as to stop passengers from standing on the front platform to smoke, it made them go to the rear platform.

The D.U.R. city cars were all built 3'9" above the rails which made them adoptable for interurban use, but made them inconvient for rapid loading and unloading. Mr. Bemis in his report recommended that future orders have the floor at least one foot lower, similar to various properties around the country, to assist in speeding up operations and reduce congestion.

MOTIVE POWER

Under the 1902 organization chart, the D.U.R. had a Superintendent of Motive Power. This division was sub-divided into three areas; power stations, motor inspections, and repair shops. Six power houses and three battery units supplied power to the total system in 1902. This did not include the Rapid Railway System nor the Ann Arbor Division, which did not come under D.U.R. control until 1902, and 1907, respectively. The city power came from stations A & B built in 1895, and located near downtown Detroit on the river front. There were two storage battery units to furnish extra power during the peak loads of the rush hours. "Battery K" located on Woodward Avenue at Cortland, was rated at a 2500 ampere capacity, and "Battery L", was on Hancock between Third and Fourth Street, with a 2000 ampere capacity. The other power plant and battery unit supplied the interurban service. A modified principal is used today by the power companies by pumping water into a reservoir and letting it out through their turbines during peak loads.

In 1910, a turbine power unit was installed at the central power station. It produced 6,600 volts A.C. which was transmitted to a sub-station at Dubois and Trombley, passed through a transformer, a synchronous convertor, and to the tracks at 600 volt D.C. But power quickly became in short supply system-wide as traffic rapidly increased so, during the intervening years the out-lying areas which mostly included the interurban system, used power purchased from Detroit Edison. The 1919 Bemis report stated the total system's power consumption consisted of 53.7% D.U.R. produced power and 46.3% Detroit Edison produced power. By this late date the power generating systems had outlived their usefullness and new funds were not available or if they were, would not be spent on new equipment as long as there was a threat of the city take over. Therefore all future power needs were contracted from Detroit Edison, the local power company.

Detroit was considered the birthplace of the storage air-brake system. Its first application was on cars of the Detroit and Pontiac Railway in 1898. Two high pressure storage reservoirs carrying 300 pounds pressure were mounted on each car. The high pressure supply was furnished by a compressor in the power station at Birmingham, the cars being charged at least once each trip.

The results were satisfactory, and by February 1905, all the double truck cars had the system installed. Air tanks on the single truck cars were being installed at the rate of 3 to 5 per day. The charging stations were provided for all lines at their respective car houses. In addition, a portable compressing unit along with necessary storage and cooling tanks were installed in a specially built box car. The car was double truck closed body type, equipped with motors and a high gear ratio for rapid traveling. The purpose of the car was to provide a charging station for emergency cases and to be used at places not continually demanding permanent compressing equipment. This was usually on a short line where only a few cars were in use. In this way the compressor car would travel to several car houses to charge their tanks and save the cost and maintenance of air-compressor equipment. All D.U.R. city cars taken over by the D.S.R. operated with storage tanks until the late 1920's when the remaining cars had air compressors installed.

This turn of the century photo shows car 441 of the Third Street line. Originally numbered in 41-55 series these cars had been purchased for the Grand River line when it was electrified. **D.S.R. Files.**

The top two photos show the open and closed versions of the Detroit platform as it was called industry wide. The bottom picture had this memo on the back "Dinkey, side collect car, aisle on avenue (right) only, reach in for fare, taking on air. Dad Reed, Trumbull Car House, Myrtle Line — 1918" **D.S.R. Files.**

Exterior and interior photos of the "Yolande", a car with many names but one purpose. First it was called "Special", then "tourist", then its most famous name the "Yolande" finally near its end, "Ottawa". It began as an excursion car visiting the tourist attractions of the city on a circular route that lasted two hours. One could board the car at any street along the route for a twenty-five cent fare. The car passed the principal wholesale district, manufacturing plants, residential, Water Works Park and Belle Isle. An attendant with the car explained the points of interest. In 1902 this car was known as "Yolande". The original single truck car with that name had returned to regular service. The last name "Ottawa" was applied when assigned the Pontiac to Detroit run for the Eastern Michigan Railway. In 1932 the car was sold to become a roadside diner at Clarkston, Mich., where it burned to the ground. **Faber Collection.**

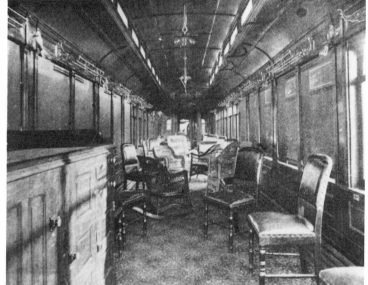

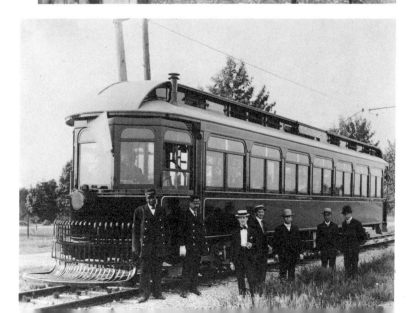

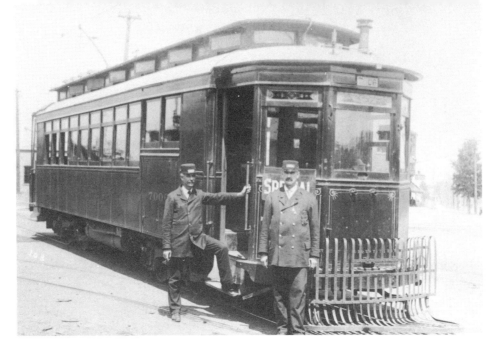

The interurban funeral cars replaced the smaller single truck funeral car which was found inadequate to handle the services to the newer suburban cemeteries. The first, 1027, which had been 7004 passenger interurban, was rebuilt as follows; the interior was divided into two compartments, the forward for the casket and the rear for the funeral party. The seating for 38 persons was green plush. The interior was finished in cherry wood with the ceiling a pale green with gold borders and stenciling, and the windows had plate glass. The exterior was black with gold stripping.

The funeral car rates in Detroit to the following cemeteries (including stops at church) were: Wood-mere, Elmwood, Mt. Elliott, German Lutheran, Crematorium and Beth-Olem-$15.00: Woodlawn, Evergreen, Forest Lawn, Mt. Olivet, Gethsemane and Beth-David-$20.00: Roseland, Grand Lawn, Grotto, Grosse Pointe, Royal Oak, Oak View and Machpalah-$25.00. Those on the interurban lines were $25.00 to $60.00.

Car 1027 went into service November 12, 1902. Two cars were added; 7006 in 1908, 7007 in 1911. These cars retained their original numbers. The photo was taken in front of Jefferson Terminal in 1912 and shows the appearance of 7007. The photo is from the John Campbell family who was the motorman in this picture.

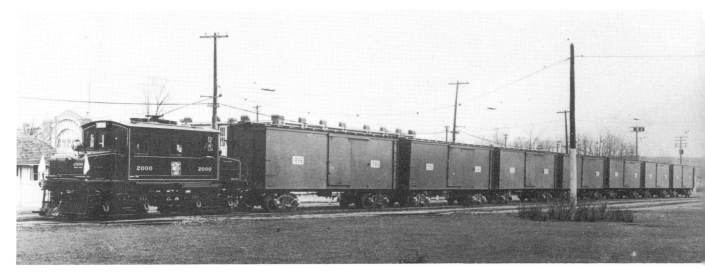

LEFT: A little known or published operation is the important job of counting the coins. Here automatic money counting machines have been placed in service at the D.U.R. in 1919. **Manning Brothers Historical Collection.** TOP: The State Fair Loop, Seven and a half mile road and Woodward, served both city passenger cars and interurban freight trains. Motor 2000 after making up a train will head up Woodward toward Flint. The interurban system will be a later volume. **Clarence Woodard Collection. CENTER RIGHT:** Snow plows on the D.U.R. came in all shapes. Here 1808 pauses from other duties on a snowless day at the Warren car house September 12, 1922. **Jack Schramm Collection. LOWER RIGHT:** Plows were used during construction work as dirt or ballast levelers. Note the method used to raise the front plow of 7805. **Jack Schramm Collection.**

Changes in rate of fare
Detroit United Railway

Date Effective	So-called 5¢ lines	So-called 3¢ lines
Prior to August 15, 1913	5¢ cash. Workingman's ticket 8 for 25¢ (good from 5 to 6 a.m. and 4:45 to 5:45 p.m.) Free transfer on 5¢ fare to 5¢ or 3¢ line and on ticket fare to 3¢ line only.	5¢ cash or 8 for 25¢ ticket (Good from 5:15 a.m. to 7:30 p.m.) or 6 for 25¢ ticket (Good from 7:30 p.m. to 5:15 a.m.) Free transfer on 5¢ fare to 3¢ or 5¢ line and on ticket fare to 3¢ line only.
August 15, 1913 A fare reduction given in lieu of paying a track rental.	5¢ cash or 7 for 25¢ ticket (good any time) Workingman's ticket as above. Free transfer on 5¢ fare or 7 for 25¢ ticket to 3¢ or 5¢ line and on 8 for 25¢ ticket to 3¢ line only	Same as above, and 7 for 25¢ ticket (good any time) Free transfer on 5¢ fare or 7 for 25¢ ticket to 3¢ or 5¢ line and on other tickets to 3¢ line only.
December 1, 1917 Put into effect after arbitration award.	5¢ cash Workingman's ticket as above. Free transfer on 5¢ fare to 3¢ or 5¢ line and on ticket afer to 3¢ lint only.	5¢ cash, 8 for 25¢ ticket as above, or 6 for 25¢ ticket as above. Free transfer on 5¢ fare to 3¢ or 5¢ line and on ticket fare to 3¢ line only.
August 8, 1918 Put into effect after strike and arbitration award.	6¢ cash or 10 for 55¢ ticket. (good any time) Free transfer to 3¢ or 5¢ line.	Same as above, 10 for 55¢ ticket also accepted, good for free transfer to 3¢ or 5¢ line.
August 13, 1918 City Ordinance reduced fares.	5¢ cash or 6 for 25¢ ticket (good any time) Workingman's ticket good from 5:00 to 6:30 a.m. and from 4:45 to 5:45 p.m.) Free transfer on 5¢ fare or 6 for 25¢ ticket to 3¢ or 5¢ line and on 8 for 25¢ ticket fare to 3¢ line only.	Same as above, also 6 for 25¢ ticket good for free transfer to 3¢ or 5¢ line.
June 12, 1919 After a strike and raise, a proposed 1¢ transfer charge to be arbitrated.	5¢ cash-Free universal transfers on both 3¢ or 5¢ lines (This ended the workingman's tickets and the Pingree 3¢ lines, the city was soon to take over and found themselves unable to operate even on a 5¢ fare).	
May 31, 1920 D.U.R. increase City went to court.	5¢ cash-1¢ transfer charge	
June 9, 1920 Court order with stub for rebate.	6¢ cash or 9 for 50¢ ticket on both 3¢ and 5¢ lines Free universal transfers on all lines.	
June 19, 1921 Detroit's last fare reduction given in lieu of rebate.	5¢ cash with 1¢ transfer charge for transfer to any D.U.R. line, and commencing December 15, 1921, transfer was good on lines operated jointly by the city and D.U.R.	

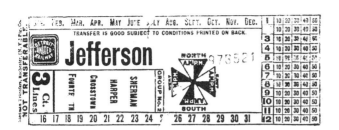

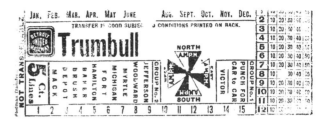

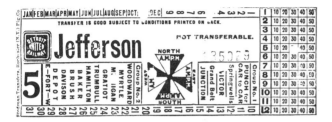

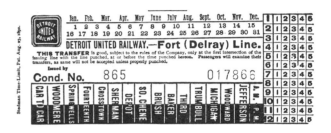

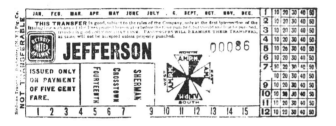

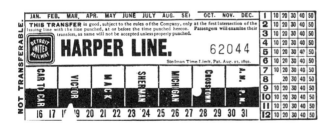

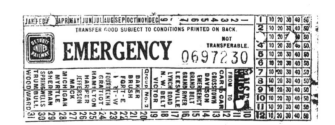

ABOVE: 1909 photo of Detroit's first large car barn built in 1879 at Woodbridge and St. Antione. It was from this building the Citizen's first electric streetcar pulled out. **Barcroft Appraisal. RIGHT:** Present appearance with the Detroit's new Renaissance Center next door. **Henning Photo.**

Power Plants A & B built in the 1890's by the D Citizens and Detroit Railways. The steeple cab car 1981, which later was rebuilt into a freight m is one of the two remaining work cars. It has restored and is operated by the Michigan Tr Museum. **Barcroft and D.U.R. photos.**

TOP: A 1909 photo of the Monroe shops at Monroe and Dequindre which were the main shops until replaced by Highland Park Shops.**Barcroft Appraisal. CENTER:** Harper Yard located at Harper and Concord where all track supplies and roadway equipment was maintained. **Faber Collection. BOTTOM:** Huge power loads occurred for an hour during the morning and evening rush hour when more than double the usual cars operated. Rather than invest in additional expensive mechanical generators, battery power was used to help move the cars. During the off peak hours the central generator charged the batteries. An example is Battery K, Woodward and Cortland Avenue, now owned by Detroit Edison. **Barcroft Appraisal.**

ABOVE: Woodward Car House torn down 1973. **D.U.R. Files . . . CENTER:** Inside typical car house. **BOTTOM:** West Jefferson Car House located near Rouge River. **Manning Brothers Historical Collection.**

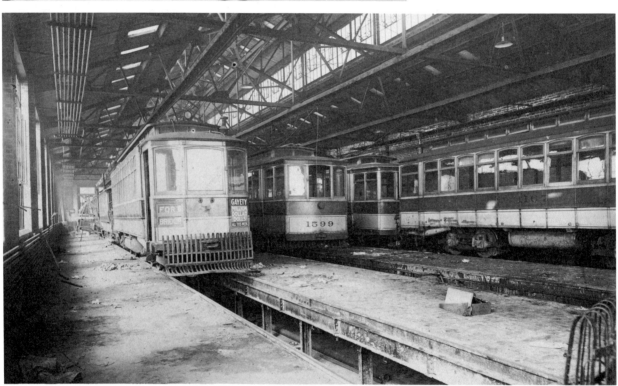

ABOVE: Woodward Terminal built about 1915. It was located directly across the street from the Ford Highland Park Plant. The terminal office building included lockers and showers on the second floor, while on the ground floor were lounging, cashier services for change and transfers, and terminal office facilities. **Schramm collection. CENTER:** Gratiot Car House originally known as Leesville Car House. **D.S.R. Files. BOTTOM:** A 1907 view of Trumbull Car House. **Faber collection.**

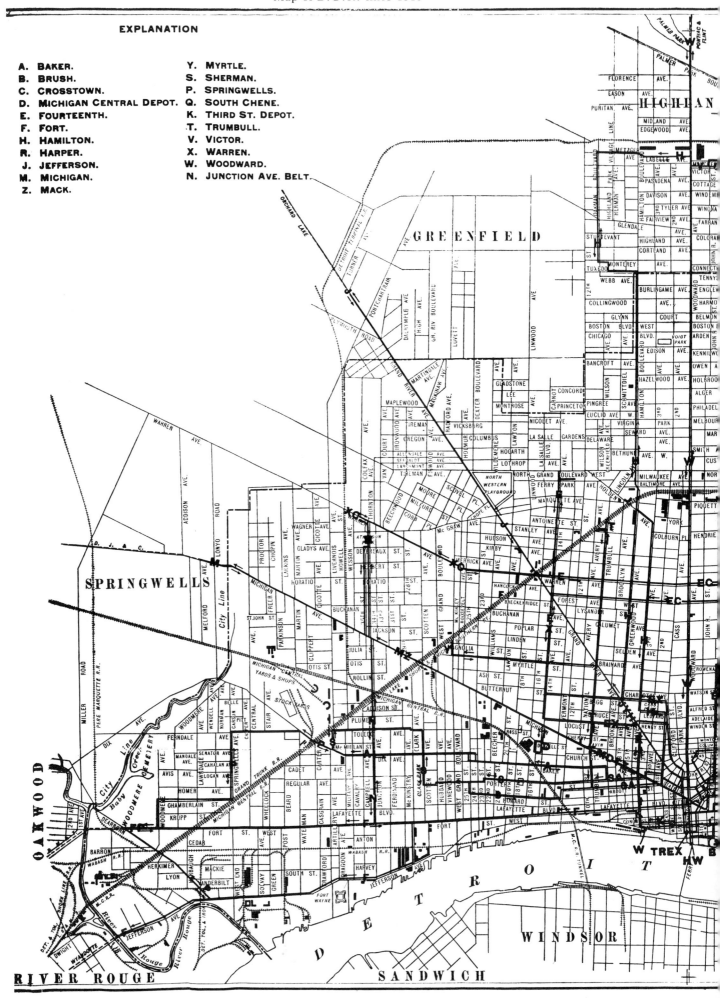

EXPLANATION

A. BAKER.
B. BRUSH.
C. CROSSTOWN.
D. MICHIGAN CENTRAL DEPOT.
E. FOURTEENTH.
F. FORT.
H. HAMILTON.
R. HARPER.
J. JEFFERSON.
M. MICHIGAN.
Z. MACK.

Y. MYRTLE.
S. SHERMAN.
P. SPRINGWELLS.
Q. SOUTH CHENE.
K. THIRD ST. DEPOT.
T. TRUMBULL.
V. VICTOR.
X. WARREN.
W. WOODWARD.
N. JUNCTION AVE. BELT.

DETROIT & SUBURBS
PRESENT STREET RAILWAY SYSTEM
ACCOMPANYING REPORT TO
BOARD OF STREET RAILWAY COMMISSIONERS
CITY OF DETROIT

BY

BARCLAY PARSONS & KLAPP, CONSULTING ENGINEERS

JANUARY, 1915

SCALE

1000   5000   10,000 Feet

RIDING THE LINES IN 1916

A European war was slowly expanding into a World War in 1916. As Detroit geared up for this war effort, the city's streetcar system reached its peak ridership. Business throughout the city was on the upswing. Yet within a few years the automobile would cut deeply into the streetcar revenue. Under the prosperous days of 1916 Matt Dean and Clarence Faber, employed by the DUR, described the characteristics of the company routes. We have selected most of their interesting descriptions.

THE BAKER LINE.

The Baker line served the newly arrived Poles in the Hamtramck and Chene-Ferry areas, the Italian district around Gratiot and Chene, the second generation of Germans at Rivard, the Irish of the Corktown district, and the second and third generation native-born Americans along Dix Avenue west of Grand Boulevard. All went to make the slogan "Dynamic Detroit; Where Life is Worth Living" a true one. This line was especially dynamic hauling the huge labor forces to and from the busy Milwaukee Junction industrial district. During the day the cars could be found carrying women shoppers to the downtown stores later brisk evening trade consisted of people going to the theatres or just visiting

The cars of the Baker line were of the 1028-1099 class recently transferred from the Woodward line when that line received newer equipment. The 1000's were always clean, elegant, and smooth running. During the peak periods the 826 to 846 class were added. These latter cars were called "bowling alleys" due to their extreme length (about 40 feet) and lengthwise seating. They had a tremendous carrying capacity; 400 fares on a one-way trip was not uncommon. Being an old Citizens line the fare was the DUR standard. Cars took on storage air at the Dix Avenue carhouse and also at the Chene Street loop. The only railroad grade crossing was on Dequindre Street with the Grand Trunk. A standard interlocking plant was used at this point.

Baker car on Michigan crossing Woodward at turn of century. **Schramm collection. BELOW:** Early Detroit with its tree shaded streets. **Schramm collection.**

ABOVE: Baker car on Michigan crossing Woodward about 1910. **Burton Historical Collection Detroit Public Library. CENTER:** Southbound on Joseph Campau at Holbrook. **Manning Brothers Historical Collection. BELOW:** Eastbound on Michigan and Cass. **Schramm collection.**

Hastings Street hosted various carlines. The 14th Street carline was a U shaped line. Its route started west of Woodward, looped through downtown and paralleled itself east of Woodward on Hastings Street. When the 14th Street route was terminated downtown a new carline, Oakland, took its place on Hastings Street. The Brush carline operated a few blocks away from Hastings Street. When it was determined that the track on Brush Street had to be renewed the Brush cars were moved to Hastings Street. This car is at Hastings and Eliot. **D.S.R. Files.**

THE BRUSH LINE.

The Brush line was just another street car line. It's only real distinction was that in summer it used open cars exclusively. This line served all the ferry boat lines between Detroit and Windsor, Canada, at the foot of Woodward Avenue, and the Canada Steamship lines at the foot of Bates Street. The Brush line also served the Grand Trunk Western Railroad depot where the street cars would be jammed at train time. On the outbound trips, the cars of this line passed the Interurban station at Jefferson and Bates. On Brush Street north of High Street (Vernor) the line served a medium income group. Around Rowena and Antoine was a mixture of Jewish, Polish, and Italian neighborhoods most of whom were employed at the Ford plant in Highland Park. Around Ferry and Russell there was a large settlement of Slavs. The DUR recruited most of their track laborers from these neighborhoods. Many passengers on this line were railroad men who rode to the New York Central and Wabash yards at Piquette and Russell. Equipment used was of the open fan-tail 1200 series. The conductor went through the car collecting the nickel fares or "Seven Fer" tickets, standard procedure on the DUR. Cars were housed at the barns on Ferry and Russell, which was where they also took on storage air for the brake tanks. In summer, cars of the 800 class were also used on this line. There were no railroad crossings and only one industrial siding into the Public Lighting Station on Atwater Street used by the Grand Trunk.

THE CROSSTOWN LINE.

The Crosstown line was principally a transfer line. When the fare boxes were emptied at night there was usually not much cash or tickets, but the conductors turned in large amounts of transfers. At this time there were no other east-west cross city routes and anyone using the main north-south lines were obliged to transfer to or from the Crosstown line. It connected with every line except a few of the outlying routes. It also connected with most of the interurban lines. The route was built as a Detroit Railway line, and as such charged the 3 cent fare during most of the day. On Sundays during the summer this line was heavily used being that it served Belle Isle Park, and the open cars were very popular. The cars were usually full despite a two-minute headway during the day and a five-minute headway in the evening. During the rush hours, two or three cars per block was a common sight. One might see westbound Crosstown cars backed up for two blocks waiting to cross Woodward Avenue. There were no traffic lights at that corner, and with the heavy street car traffic on Woodward it was indeed a busy crossing. Crosstown cars were of the 900-class, pay-as-you-enter, and single-truck. Lengthwise seats held 30 passengers. Storage air was obtained at the Warren and Kercheval car houses. There were no industrial sidings on the line but there was considerable interurban freight movement and work car traffic which by using the Crosstown tracks could avoid the downtown area.

The Crosstown line was developed by the Detroit Railway Company in 1896. Their cars had a center entrance with seats opposite the door side of the car.

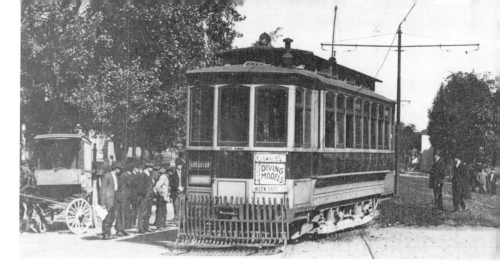

The bucking characteristics of single truck (four wheels) cars created numerous derailments, such as this one on the Crosstown Line. This rough ride problem helped persuade the management to phase out the single truck cars. Unfortunately, rough riding and small carrying capacity was also true for the Birney cars ordered later by the city. **Burton Historical Collection.**

DEPOT LINE

The Depot line connected all the railroad stations and steamship docks, including the Interurban Building at Bates and Jefferson. The route was as follows; commencing at the 15th Street entrance of the Michigan Central Station, then south on single track to Marantette to 14th. to Michigan, to double track, to Third, then south on single track to Jefferson, to Griswold, to Atwater to Brush location of Brush Street Grand Trunk Railroad depot. Then north on Brush to Jefferson to Griswold returning to Michigan Depot. The fare was the standard D.U.R. and the cars were of the open fan tail 300 and 400 types. The conductor walked through the cars to collect the fares which he rang up on the fare register "sometimes".

Cars loaded patrons at the Michigan Central depot on three tracks now the depot parking lot. Track one was used by the Depot Line. Woodward and Michigan cars loaded on the second track, while the third track was used by Flint and Mt. Clemens interurban's which met the morning trains from the east and south. These interurbans went directly to their destinations not going by the Interurban Building.

During the baseball season track #3 and unused street tracks were used to store trippers needed to carry fans home from Navin Field. Third Street from Michigan to Congress Streets was used also by interurban freight cars to reach the Electric Depot and a passing track was located at Howard Street.

Cars ran from 6:00 a.m. to 8:00 p.m. and were manned by Michigan West crews. Service was about 5 minutes headway and storage air was taken from a compressor station on Marantette Street just west of the alley between 14th and 15th. Depot cars carried only a Depot sign on the celestory with no destination signs.

DEARBORN ROAD LINE

A free line was operated on Dearborn Ave. from West Jefferson to Fort Street, being single tracked to Fort St. with a turn-out at Melville Ave. Cars returned over the same route. An occasional car operated over the Rouge Bridge on Fort St. into the village of Oakwood. The purpose of this being to maintain the franchise in Oakwood Village. It was a two-man double-end operation using single truck cars numbered 311 and 377 which were housed at the Clark Avenue car house.

From the late 1800's to 1914 both the Michigan Central depot and the Union depot (Right) were located a few blocks apart on Third Street. This view of Third Street from Fort looking towards the river have other buildings obscuring the M.C. depot next to the river. With the completion of the railroad tunnel the Michigan Central depot was moved to Michigan and 14th Street. **Manning Brothers Historical Collection.**

On the west bank of the River Rouge on the Fort Street Bridge. This was the interurban bridge which at the time of the photo was being used by automobile traffic while a new bridge was being constructed. **Dworman Collection.**

THE FORT LINE.

The Fort Line had two separate terminals. The Delray and River Rouge portion was double-tracked from the downtown area at Cadillac Square west along Fort Street to Clark, south to West Jefferson and west again to a loop at the River Rouge Bridge. Certain cars ran over the bridge and continued to South Dearborn Avenue (now Coolidge). During rush hours some cars carried a sign "Fort-Great Lakes". This was a single track line which branched off of West Jefferson and looped in front of the Great Lakes Engineering Works. There was one industrial siding on West Jefferson into the Detroit Edison plant. There were numerous railroad crossings which made for erratic service. One of these crossings was the scene of a tragic accident on April 15, 1915. City car 1502 was torn to pieces when it was struck by a D.T.&I. train. An unusual series of events led to this mishap. The car stopped about 50 feet short of the crossing to discharge passengers and to permit the conductor to flag the car through the diamond. The conductor signalled the car to come ahead, but before it cleared the crossing it stopped unexpectedly to permit another passenger to alight. A 25 car train of pig iron was being pushed across the swing bridge connecting Zug Island. The student motorman started the car and would have cleared the train, but the motorman instructor along side of him didn't think he would try to beat the train and threw the controller in reverse. The car stopped, straddling the crossing. The engineer's vision was cut off by the bridge trusses and the car was struck amidships. 1502 was pushed far down the railroad right-of-way causing damge to several adjacent buildings. Sixteen people were killed in the DUR's worst accident.

Intersection at Fort and Clark Streets in 1916. **Manning Brothers Historical Collection.**

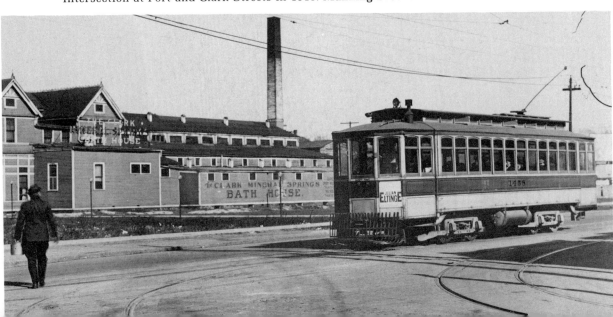

Another view of the intersection at Fort and Clark Streets in 1916. **Manning Brothers Historical Collection.**

The Fort-Woodmere (or Through) line started at Baldwin and East Lafayette, ran through downtown, and out Fort Street to a loop at Dearborn Street. Cars on this line were of the 1100 and 1200 class, with other series filling in when needed. Most cars were stored at the Clark Street carhouse with a few kept at Jefferson carhouse.

West Jefferson Car House turning loop at the end of the line of the Fort-Delray division. The interurbans use these tracks too. Cars destined for Wyandotte used the West Jefferson route, while the cars heading toward Toledo rolled over the Fort-Through tracks. **Schramm Collection.**

FOURTEENTH LINE.

The Fourteenth line was one where a passenger could get a transfer from a northbound car to a southbound car, because for many blocks the line ran on separate streets. The cars served a white collar, medium income neighborhood along 14th Street on the west side. East side cars ran through areas populated with Jewish, Italians, Polish, and Lithuanians. Fourteenth was a loop or belt line and the cars would carry signs with "Belt Line Up 14th" or "Belt Line Up Hastings". Due to close clearances along the

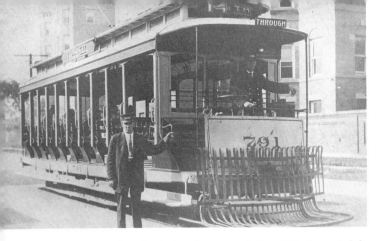

way only single-truck cars of the 600 class (nick-named Ponchatrain) were used. In the summer the open-type 800 series cars were added.

There was a branch line on Clay Street which operated as a free shuttle. This short line ran from early morning to late at night using one-man single-truck cars. Considerable freight moved over this section. There was a five car train yard, located just north of Clay at the Grand Trunk Railroad. Auto bodies bound for Flint and Pontiac were loaded here.

A new motorman or conductor on the 14th line had an obnoxious job until he accumulated considerable seniority. The line served the Ford plant and new men would have to make an early morning trip, another during the afternoon, and still another around eleven at night. During shift changes there would be an average of three cars per block all the way downtown.

Storage air was taken on at Warren and 14th, and at Woodland and Oakland. Some took on air at 14th and Forest where an underground tank was located. The tank was filled daily by a special car, numbered 1000. There were a number of railroad grade crossings and the industrial spur at Clay Street. One more spur led into the Gable (later McDonald) Creamery. This was used by a milk car from the Flint Division of the DUR at the Atlas station for delivery.

ABOVE: A turn of the century photo on the 14th line. **Schramm collection. LEFT:** At the time of this photo the 14th line ended at Grand Boulevard. The line was extended to Six Mile Road much later. **Faber collection. BELOW:** In 1914 the camera caught this rare picture of a 14th open bench car crossing Michigan. **Manning Brothers Historical Collection.**

THE "FERRY LOOP" BY CHARLES PETCHER

Although today on the D.S.R. it is not possible to transfer from one bus to another on the same line except in case of emergency or a change from local to express bus and vice-versa, the Detroit United Railway early in the century operated the 14th. trolley route on which one could transfer at Capitol Park from a car, bound for the 14th Ferry Park terminus, to a car bound for the Oakland-Woodland terminus.

The 14th Ferry Park terminus was on the upper West side and the Oakland-Woodland one was in the old north end. After arriving at Capitol Park, 14th

ABOVE: Hastings and Forest. **Manning Brothers Historical Collection. BELOW:** An early electric on Oakland at Josephine in 1918. **Manning Brothers Historical Collection.**

"Through" cars, bound for Oakland-Woodland made a loop via Shelby, West Jefferson, Griswold, East and West Woodbridge, Bates and Farmer before resuming the regular route at Gratiot and Farmer. This loop was known as the "Ferry Loop" because it served the Windsor and Belle Isle ferry docks. Cars in the opposite direction did not follow the loop. From Gratiot and Farmer they continued west via Gratiot and State to Capitol Park, Later "Ferry Loop" cars operated via Griswold, West Jefferson East Jefferson Bates and Farmer.

Passengers bound for the boat dock area could board a 14th car in the North end and, upon payment of a blue workingman's ticket receive a free "Ferry Loop" transfer. The "Ferry Loop" is almost forgotten today. It does revivie memories of a Detroit, then expanding beyond the Grand Boulevard, whose people enjoyed Belle Isle band concerts, visits to Riverview Park and trips on excursion steamers.

THE GRATIOT LINE

The Gratiot line was just street car transportation, but it must have been one of the best paying D.U.R. lines because of the short distance it travelled, and the loads of people that it carried. There was no fast running streetcars on the Gratiot line, and every car made nearly every stop from Woodward to Leesville, (now Gratiot and Harper). Your authors very seldom took a fan trip on it and then the only satisfaction we got was to sit in the front of the car and see an inbound or outbound 7300 interurban on the Mt. Clemens-Port Huron division passby.

The Gratiot line was a double track and the route was as follows: From Leesville car house at Gratiot and Harper west on Gratiot to Randolph, to Monroe, to Michigan, to Griswold to Congress, to Woodward, to Monroe then eastward over the same route. Being a D.U.R. route the fare was standard. Cars were of the 1600 double truck, two motor pay as you enter type.

Service was about three minutes during the day and at rush hour they ran almost bumper to bumper. Cars of the Rapid Division, interurbans to Port Huron, used the Gratiot line tracks also and the dispatchers phone booth on that division was located at Gratiot and Harper on the northeast corner. Inbound crews from Mt. Clemens and Port Huron also registered in here. There were no industrial spurs, but a four track yard was located at Gratiot and Superior. Due to the proximity of most of the brewerys, much beer was loaded here for Flint and

Gratiot and Riopelle a section of the Gratiot line shared with the Mack line. **Public Lighting Commission files.**

Pontiac which were local option towns, also automobile bodies from Everett Bros. on Beaufait and Mack, which were shipped to Toledo, Flint and Pontiac. We would mention here that all these shipments were hauled by horses and wagons because at that time there were not over 50 motor trucks in the whole city. Even Fisher Body Company had many horses and wagon for cartage.

Something else we should mention at this time and was common on the D.U.R. was called "switch boys". These were boys from 13 to 16 years old who stood at important streetcar intersections and with a switch-bar and turned the switch for whichever way the car was bound. One of the busiest ones we recall was at Jefferson and Woodward and the southwest corner where the Jefferson and Woodward cars separated and the next was at Woodward and Monroe where the Woodward, Hamilton, Brush Gratiot lines diverted. Others were stationed at Grand River and Woodward, also at the southwest and northwest corner of Griswold and Michigan. Boys hired for this work received 15 cents per hour and two "Dago" passes each day. "Dago" passes were slips of paper given to Italian gandy dancers employed by the company for transportation from and to the job each day. They were similar to the duplex tickets used on the interurban lines being in two sections. When the employee presented it to the conductor he punched it and returned half of it to the rider who in turn returned it or five cents to his supervisor the next day. The theory was, that the employee might sell the pass for four cents, buy a glass of beer and walk home.

Gratiot cars were housed at Leesville car house and storage air was taken at the car house and also Mack and Gratiot. A standard Railroad interlocking plant took the cars over the Grand Trunk at Dequindre and the Michigan Central Belt Line at Beaufait.

THE HAMILTON LINE

While the Hamilton line was just another line, a juice fan would ride it perhaps more than some D.U.R.

Lines as it had some private right-of-way running. Some side and center of the road tracks were used, and several interurban-type switches might be seen along the route.

It served a working class of people along Third Avenue and Greenwood Avenue (Hamilton) from Grand Avenue to Warren Avenue, and a middle class of people north from Warren to Highland Park. A large number of the newly arrived English and Scotch immigrants lived near the intersection of Hamilton and LaBelle. They made up a large number of the riders on the Hamilton line.

The route of the Hamilton line was as follows: On the private right-of-way at the intersection opposite Victor Avenue and Woodward Avenue, it was double track west on the private right of way to Hamilton Boulevard thence a short jog north on Hamilton. Then to Metzger (Oakman Boulevard). Oakman Boulevard (now Woodrow Wilson) to a point just north of Elmhurst at the rear of the Detroit Tuberculosis Hospital, then east to Herman Avenue to Webb to Hamilton, thence south on Hamilton Boulevard to Holden, single track on Holden to Third to Ledyard to Cass. Thence double track on Grand River to Woodward Avenue to single track on Atwater Street to Brush Street Depot. The north bound route was north on Brush to Jefferson to Woodward to Grand River to single track on Greenwood (later Hamilton, now John C. Lodge expressway) to the intersection of Holden where Greenwood became Hamilton, then northbound over the same route as southbound.

The cars were of the low 1100 hundred double truck two-motor type and were pay-as-you-enter. Later in 1916 some of the new 3000 type steel cars and trailers were used as trippers. All freight cars for the Flint and Pontiac divisions of the D.U.R. coming to and from the electric depot at 5th. and Congress used the Hamilton line as did all the cars from the west side going to the Highland Park shops for repairs. These cars switched off the Hamilton line at the northwest corner of Hamilton and Oakman Blvd. The extension of the Hamilton line on Hamilton north to Six Mile Road was not built until the latter part of 1917.

The Hamilton line being a D.U.R. line had a five cent fare. A physical connection was made with the Detroit Terminal Railroad just west of Hamilton. It was used to set out gondolas of coal for the T.B. Sanitorium on Elmhurst which had a spur track running to the rear of the boiler house.

Hamilton cars carried the signs "Hamilton'River" southbound, northbound the cars marked, "Hamilton-House turned at the car house at Greenwood and Holden. "Hamilton-Pingree" wyed at Pingree, and cars going to the end of the line carried "Hamilton-Through".

Storage air was taken on at the northern terminus, and at Hamilton Car house at Greenwood and Holden. With the exception of a few runs out of Woodward car house all cars were housed at Holden Ave. The line was lightly patronized and, except rush hours, one could always get a seat.

THE HARPER LINE

If the average trolley fan of today were to be transported back to 1916 he would say of the Harper line "In all the world no line is like this". One could board the Harper line in downtown Detroit and in 45 minutes be watching a farmer plow or harvest his grain. It travelled the most narrow and congested streets in Detroit and the farm country of Macomb County which was as remote from Detroit as the farm lands of Iowa. On Harper one could see every type of equipment the D.U.R. owned. Construction cars, freight cars, interurbans, line cars, shop cars, in other words you name it, you would see it. One would even see on Bates and Congress Streets a northbound "Dinkey" sandwiched in between a couple Lake Shore electrics hooked M.U. bound for Cleveland and a big 800 of the Michigan Railway all waiting for a 1200 on the Myrtle line to clear the diamond at Bates and Congress.

The city route of the Harper line started at Harper and Van Dyke on single track running on the north side of Harper Ave. to Frontenac switch, then on double track center of street operation to Mt. Elliott to Hendricks, single track on Hendricks to Jos Campau, to Sherman, to Hastings, to Clinton, to Brush, to Macomb, to Gratiot, to State, to Shelby, to Jefferson, to Bates, to Farmer returning via Gratiot, to Macomb, to Russell, to Catherine(Madison) to Jos Campau north to Waterloo to Mt. Elliott thence over the same route as the west bound route.

At the end of the Hamilton line at Webb in 1912 when it was still named Third. **Dworman collection. BELOW:** Hamilton and Delaware. **Manning Brothers Historical Collection.**

THE CENTERLINE ROUTE

The Centerline route continued north on Van Dyke to a loop just north of Ten Mile road. The stretch of track from Harper to Ten Mile Road is one where we made many fan trips as this was the only interurban running our pass book was valid on. This segment of the line was open running side of road operation on the east side of Van Dyke. A passing switch was located just north of the Detroit Terminal Railroad, a long spur at Conner's Creek and east of Van Dyke was where all the rubbish collected on the D.U.R. city lines was dumped. Conners Creek was crossed on an iron girder bridge such as the railroads cross the River Rouge today. This bridge over Conners Creek was located about where Dubay Street is now. Conners Creek was navigable to small boats at that time and adventurous people would rent a canoe at Belle Isle and paddle across the River, then up Conners Creek to the vicinity of 8 Mile Road and Mound. A loop was located just north of 6 Mile Road at Mt. Olivet Cemetery and passing tracks were at Seven, Eight, Nine, and Ten Mile Roads.

On Sundays during the summer there was a picnic grove on the site of Currier Lumber Co. with many extra cars run from Forest and Mt. Elliott to the Mt. Olivet Loop. There were no dispatchers or phone at

Harper and the Boulevard — 1919. **Manning Brothers Historical Collection.**

these loops or passing tracks and on a Sunday these cars would sometimes meet in between passing tracks and the sections that had the fewest cars would back up to a switch and let the others pass.

Open cars were used to the fullest extent on Sundays but many other single truck type cars were used. One of the favorite fan trips was to board a Harper-Center Line car at Bates and Jefferson and ride out to Center Line then return to Railroad (Nevada). Then walk to the village of Norris which was at Mt. Elliott and Railroad., board a Norris car to the Tyler Street Wye, (Council) in Hamtramck, walk across the railroad, then board a Baker car at the loop for a trip back downtown. The Harper line fare was 8 tickets for 25¢ during the day.

Service was about 3 minutes during the day and one car followed another during rush hours. Cars left downtown for the cemeteries on the half hour and on the hour for Center Line. Cars were of the "Pingree" or 100 to 175 series with an entrance in the side as well as the front and rear. Some single truck 400's also 1200's of the low series were used. Open cars were largely used during the summer, also a few "Ponchar-trains" or 600's. Cars going to Center Line at night were wired for arc lights and the Center Line cars met at Frontenac switch were the arc light was transferred to the outbound cars from the inbound. This

light was known by the crews as the "eye".

Cars crossed the Grand Trunk at Sherman and Catherine Streets by a derail lever operated by the conductor. The Michigan Central Belt line was crossed by the standard railroad interlocking plant and over the Detroit Terminal the conductor flagged the car across and the Grand Trunk on Van Dyke was crossed by an outside two lever interlocker operated by the conductor. The semaphore was always set for the steam road, so each conductor had to get out and "decorate". Storage air was taken on only at Harper yards and the cars were housed at Leesville car house.

LEESVILLE LINE

The Leesville line was a connecting line that ran from Harper and Gratiot to Van Dyke and Harper. It was single track open running side of road operation with a passing track at about Seneca Ave. The fare was standard D.U.R. Cars were of the "Ponchar-train" or 600 series and were housed at Leesville. Service was about 20 minutes at all times. This line carried few passengers and was used mostly by Harper cars going to and from Leesville car house and construction cars coming in and going out over the Port Huron Division.

Overcrowded cars were typical of rush hours as workers tried to get home. The city used scenes like this to push for city ownership. Harper "plug" at Mt. Elliot and Boulevard. **Schramm Collection.**

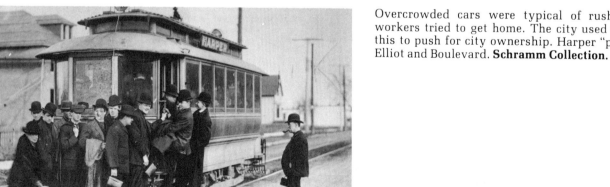

JEFFERSON LINE (JEFFERSON GRAND RIVER)

The Jefferson line patrons were divided into two groups. To a large extent the Jefferson section was the "Carriage Trade", while the Grand River section might be called the "White Collar Folks". Jefferson Ave. in 1916 from Hastings to Cadillac, with the exception of a few blocks from Mt. Elliott to Sheridan was lined with the homes of the well to do, while the streets northwest of Trumbull and north of Grand River were peopled with the small businessman, and so-called junior executives of their Jefferson Ave. employers.

Jefferson Ave. cars never ran with flat wheels and were always kept freshly varnished and appeared to have been washed each day. This may have been due to the fact that the lovable Jere Hutchins who was then chairman of the board of directors maintained an "apartment at the Pasedena Apartments at Jefferson and McDougal, and the "Austere President" Frank Brooks had a home at Van Dyke and Jefferson. Mr. Hutchins also had a country home in Grosse Pointe. While these two men were brothers-in-law they were two opposites in that while Brooks

Leesville line at Harper and Seminole, 1920 showing D.U.R. track construction stopped by city. **Manning Brothers Historical Collection. BELOW:** Grand River and Cass on a dark February day 1921. **Detroit Edison**

preferred his chauffer driven car, most every morning Hutchins could be found on his way to the office behind the motorman violating a company rule. Behind each motorman was a sign which read "No talking to Motorman" and someone would usually add, "He is dead from the neck up anyway" or something similar. If Hutchins did not know the motorman when he boarded, he did when he got off.

The city route of the Jefferson line was west on Jefferson from a loop at Wayburn Ave. to Griswold, north to Grand River and northwest on Grand River to a loop at Dumbarton Road. Cars returned over the same route except eastbound cars ran on the west side of Griswold Grand River to State. all the line was double track, except the portion at Capitol Park.

Westbound cars carried the sign "Jefferson-Grand River" and eastbound car "Jefferson-Field" which wyed at Field and Jefferson. "Jefferson-House"

Building the Belle Isle viaduct under Jefferson Avenue 1920. **Manning Brothers Historical Collection.**

which terminated at Jefferson Car House. "Jefferson-Limits" which looped at Wayburn loop. "Jefferson-Grosse Pointe" which wyed at Fisher Road, "Jefferson-Gaukler Pointe" which looped at Gaukler Pointe (Ford Estate).

City crews operated the cars that ran out to Fisher Road, but Rapid Railway crews operated the cars from Fisher Road to Gaukler Pointe exchanging cars with the city crews at Fisher Road. The fare from Fisher Road to Gaukler Pointe was 15¢ and from Wayburn to Fisher 5¢ which was deposited in a container passed around by the conductor, while on the Fisher Gaukler section the conductor collected the fare and issued a duplex receipt.

Without exception all Jefferson cars were 1500's double truck pay-as-you-enter. Orchard Lake division cars used the Grand River portion of this line and Lake Shore division to Mt. Clemens the Jefferson Portion. Storage air was taken on at the Jefferson Car House, Wayburn loop, Field and Jefferson and Trumbull and Grand River.

The standard railroad interlocking plant was located at the Detroit Terminal Railroad and east Jefferson. An industrial siding into the Chalmers Motor Car Company just east of the D.T.R.R. tracks led off the eastbound tracks., also a physical connection with the Detroit Terminal Railroad off the eastbound track west of the interlocking plant.

A long siding extended nearly to the river at the east side of Water Works Park from the east bound track. Construction cars could pick-up the cars at the Terminal Railroad connection and haul them to Water Works Park and then shove them into the long siding to be unloaded. Later, construction cars would pull them out against the flow of traffic on the eastbound rails until they got them all out on Jefferson, then two more construction cars which had been waiting on the eastbound track east of the siding would couple on and with two pulling and two shoving they would return to the terminal connection, then the two that were pulling would cut off, a terminal engine would reach out to the trolley rails with a couple of flats or idlers, pull them onto the terminal rails.

Turning off Wier Lane onto Kercheval. **Motorman Robert Peake's Family Photo.**

On Mack with its fancy light poles at Garland. **Manning Brothers Historical Collection.**

MICHIGAN-MACK LINE

The "Michigan-Mack" line as it was called by 1916 standards the nearest thing to Rapid Transit. The cars were fast and comfortable to ride in. Car number 1783 was timed at 32 miles per hour between Martin andLonyo Road. There was very little vehicle traffic on either Mack or Michigan as both streets ended in the mud at the city limits, so this made for fast running. About the only slow portions of the line was from Chene and Gratiot to the city hall as it shared this part of the route with the Baker and Brush lines, and from the City Hall west to 14th. where this part was used jointly with the Sherman, Trumbull, Depot, Baker and the Michigan Depot section of the Woodward line. The D.J.&C interurban division of the D.U.R. also used the section from Griswold to Addison switch. The route was as follows: double track in both directions, west on Mack from the loop at Hart to Gratiot, to Randolph, to Monroe, to Michigan, to a Wye on the north side of Michigan between Addison and Homedale Streets. Eastbound

the route was the same.

The fare was the standard D.U.R. fare. The cars were of the 1700 double truck pay as you enter type, but did not have folding rear doors as the other pay as you enter type. The conductor stood in a more or less exposed place with sliding doors separating him from the passenger section. As these cars were fast, some were equipped with arc lights and air whistles and were used in the summer time on Sundays on the Mt. Clemens Shore Line Divison of the Rapid Railway, to handle the extra crowds that went trolley riding for a past time. Service was about three minutes in the day and about five minutes at night, with owl cars after midnight. The main barn of the Mack line was at Michigan and Military, with a few housed at Leesville and known as Michigan East. Westbound cars carried the signs "Michigan-Through". Eastbound cars carried only a "Mack" route sign and no destination sign. Cars took on storage air at the Michigan car house and at Hart Loop.

A standard railroad interlocking plant carried the

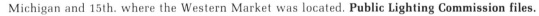

Michigan and 15th. where the Western Market was located. **Public Lighting Commission files.**

cars over the Grand Trunk at Gratiot and Dequindre and over the Michigan Central R.R. Belt line at Beaufait. Cars were flagged over the Pere Marquette Railroad at Michigan and Military by the conductors. There were no industrial sidings and no steam road connections. However, a three track yard was located at the wye at Addison, the tracks running off the north leg of the wye held about 8 Detroit, Jackson and Chicago maintenance of way or freight cars, which were brought over from Harper yards by construction car crews. Later in 1916 the dispatchers phone booth was moved to Wyoming Road and a single track built on the east side of Wyoming and north of Michigan which held 40 cars, part of this track later served the Desoto Plant. Westbound trains were made up in the early evening for Jackson and west, and arriving trains broken up in the morning for various yards in the city and at Electric Depot at Fifth and Congress.

The Michigan line served Navin Field and many trippers were run on the days when the Detroit Tigers were at home, this being the days when Ty Cobb, Walter Johnson and Babe Ruth were in their prime. Indeed, the Michigan-Mack line was pure streetcar transportation.

THE NORRIS LINE.

The Norris line. was built as a real estate promotion to the village of Norris later called North Detroit. When first built the line was semi-interurban in nature, but as the area grew the line was all inside the city. The village of Norris was located where Nevada and Mt. Elliott Avenues intersect. The line had no physical connection with any other rail line. The cars on the line were "orphans". Whenever it was necessary to bring one in for repairs to the Highland Park shops trackmen laid portable sections of track across the Grand Trunk, Michigan Central, and Detroit Terminal tracks. A shop car with a long cable pulled the car to the Baker line tracks where it was re-railed. When the car was returned, the procedure was reversed, but this time the other car on the Norris line pulled it back home again. The two cars that ran on the line in the daytime passed at the Davison and Joseph Campau switch. At night only one car operated. Fare was five cents straight and no transfers were issued to the Baker line. Storage air was taken on at the Council "Wye" being piped from the compressor station at the Chene loop. Cars were scheduled to meet the Michigan Central's train from Bay City which stopped at the Norris Station. These cars were ex-Wyandotte interurbans. Eventually the Baker line tracks were extended across the maze of tracks and the Norris line as such became part of the larger line.

North Detroit car taken in 1919 on Mt. Elliott at Nevada. **Manning Brothers Historical Collection.**

SHERMAN LINE

It was said no one ever rode the Sherman line unless he was compelled to. People on the east side preferred to walk an extra block to Jefferson or north to the fast Mack line when they wished to come downtown. On the west side they used the Fort on the south or the Baker line on the north. The Sherman line was the butt of almost as many jokes as the 14th. line, as it meandered all over, but it got to its destinations. If one made a round trip on the Sherman line, one would ride 27 Detroit streets and on this ride one would meet cars of the Crosstown, Harper, 14th., Jefferson, Myrtle, Orchard Lake Division interurbans, Trumbull, Michigan, Mack, D.J.C. interurbans, Baker, Woodward, Depot, and Springwells using the same tracks as the Sherman line. The route was interesting one because a person could see the Irish of Corktown, the Greek settlements around Brush and Macomb, a few colored people around Rivard Street, some Italian's on Russell, many Germans on Jos Campau and many Belgians out Kercheval.

The route of the Sherman line was as follows: From a Wye at St. Jean and Kercheval west on double track to Mt. Elliott, north on Hendricks, west on single track to Jos Campau, south to Sherman, to Hastings, to Clinton, to Brush, to Macomb, which was double track to Gratiot, to State, to Shelby, to Michigan and then on single track on Porter as far as 24th. where double track began again, continuing west to Scotten, to Toledo, to Livernois, to Dix, east a very short distance to a loop at Baker Car House, located at Dix and Dragoon. Eastbound the route was west on Dix, to Livernois, to Toledo to Scotten, to 24th., then on single track to Howard, to 12th., to Abbott, to Michigan, on single track on Cass, to State, to Gratiot, to Macomb again on single track, to Russell, to Catherine, to Jos. Campau, to Waterloo, to Mt. Elliott, then over the same route as eastbound. The Sherman being a Pingree three cent line one could ride for one 8 for 25¢ ticket until 8:00 p.m. and obtain a free transfer to other Pingree lines, Crosstown, 14th Harper, a regular D.U.R. fare entitled a free transfer to all D.U.R. lines.

The standard car of the line was 851 to 899 series cars. These cars were well kept up and had seats on each side running lengthwise of the car and were covered with green carpeting. Cars were housed at Kercheval Car House at Kercheval and Concord which they shared with the Crosstown line cars. The balance were housed at Baker Car House. Storage air was taken on at both car houses.

UPPER: An unusual photo of a Sherman line car awaiting in front of a sprinkling car. **Schramm collection.**
LOWER: A cold wintery day as a east bound Springwells car on Howard passes 14th. in 1921. **Manning Brothers Historical Collection.**

An open bench car on the Trumbull line advertising baseball today. The old Trumbull line passed Navin Field home of the Detroit Tigers. **Manning Brothers Historical Collection.**

SPRINGWELLS LINE

The Springwell line was a connecting line joining the Fort-Woodmere line with the Baker-Sherman line and serving part of the village of Springwells. The line began at Dix Car House, west on single track on Dix, (Vernor), to Ferndale (Vernor), double track on Ferndale, to Springwells, then east side of road single track to Chamberlain, then south side of road operation to Woodmere, to center of street double track operation on Fort to Dearborn loop. Eastbound cars returned the same route. A passing switch was located at the southwest corner of Springwells and Chamberlain.

The cars were of the 600 or Ponchartrain type with open cars being used in the summer time. Three cars were operated during the day with trippers off the Baker line during the rush hours and cars were stored at Baker car house and operated by Baker line crews. Service was poor on account of the grade crossings of the NYC and Wabash at Dix Ave. this being the main yards of the Wabash at this time. Cars were flagged over the railroads by the crossing watchman. Storage air was taken on at Baker Car House and Dearborn Loop. This was a standard D.U.R. line.

THE TRUMBULL LINE

The Trumbull line was just another trolley line. The cars seemed to meander downtown and then they came back. We cannot recall a Trumbull car travelling very fast. About the only distinction about the Trumbull was that it served as a heavy carrying line for people who transferred to it from the Grand River and Crosstown lines who's ultimate destination was Navin Field (Tiger Stadium).

The route of the line was as follows: Except for the Congress-Shelby section all was double track. Commencing at the Trumbull Car House at the N.Y.C.R.R. and Trumbull, the cars travelled south on Trumbull to Michigan to Griswold, to Congress, to Shelby, to Larned, and then back over the same route.

The cars were low numbered 1100 and 1200 series, two motor, double truck cars. They were kept in good condition, but the roadbed on Trumbull could have been better as it was laid with grooved rail, which was suitable for single truck cars but not for eight wheelers. Storage air was taken on at the car house, also at Grand River and Trumbull, if they needed more on the return trip from downtown. The line was a standard D.U.R. line.

VICTOR LINE

The Victor line was the connecting line between the Woodward Avenue line at Woodward and Victor, and the 14th line at Woodland and Oakland. Ford's automotive plant move to Highland Park in 1909 from Detroit necessitated a method of moving massive amounts of workers who lived near the old plant to the new site each work shift. The Victor line, built totally within Highland Park, opened in 1911 helped to alleviate the congestion on the Woodward line. The route of the Victor line was as follows: North from Oakland and Woodland to the Highland Park car house on Woodward. The return route was the same with double track all the way. The portion from Connecticut and Oakland north to Victor was open running on the east side of Oakland Blvd. There was no paving on Oakland at that time.

The fare was the D.U.R. standard. Cars were of the 1400 double truck four motor type, and were equipped with arc lights, and a whistle such as used on the interurban divisions. There were no steam road crossings but there was an industrial siding into the Maxell Motor Company plant at Oakland and Rhode Island streets. When this plant was operating, several cars of parts were loaded each day for Muncie, Ind., which was the site for another plant. These cars were hauled by the D.U.R. and then handed over to some connecting electric line for their destination. The Vitor line cars were all housed at the Woodward Car House. Storage air was taken on at the car house and also at Woodland Wye.

A 1921 view of Campus Martius. **Manning Brothers Historical Collection.**

WOODWARD LINE

In all probability, there were no streetcar lines that could equal the Woodward line from the standpoint of service, cleanliness of cars and personnel. The D.U.R. hired only those applicants who met high standards of neatness, intelligence, and a pleasant personality. This could be done as trainmen held seniority on the line for which they were hired. There was no system wide senority. The Woodward cars were kept in top mechanical condition and were carefully cleaned. The newest cars of the double truck, four motor type, were always assigned to the line, afterwards were reassigned to other lines as still more modern cars were purchased.

Except for "owl" cars, all Woodward cars ran in trains — a motor car and a trailer. However, during State Fair week in September, about every type of rolling stock owned by the D.U.R. could be seen carrying passengers to the Fair Grounds. Even some double truck 1200 series from the Trumbull line, and single truck open fan tail 1200 and 1300 series from both the Brush and Myrtle lines. Sandwiched in what seemed a solid line of cars would be the Pontiac and Flint interurbans.

Except for snow plows in winter and shop cars 281 and 283 (wreckers), no non-revenue cars were permitted to use the Woodward line. Freight cars for Pontiac, Flint or Bay City used the Hamilton line to Highland Park Shops and then ran north on Woodward. Construction cars used the 14th. and Victor line to reach Highland Park Shops thus the Woodward line was for passengers only.

The woodward line was heavily used as it served the Ford Plant in Highland Park where all the Ford automobiles were manufactured at the time. River Rouge was only a swamp then! The route of the Woodward line was; South on Woodward from the loop at Log Cabin Park (Palmer Park) to Jefferson Ave. to a wye at Third and West Jefferson Ave. About every fifth train ran to the Michigan Central Depot on 15th Street, and their southbound route was from Woodward west on Congress Street to Griswold and Michigan to 14th. Street to Dazell Street to 15th. Street and return via Marionette to 14th. Street and back over the same route.

These cars carried the route and destination signs of "Michigan Depot" southbound and the regular Woodward sign northbound. Southbound Woodward

Looking north on Woodward from Campus Martius taken before the automobile era. **Schramm collection.**

UPPER: After the automobile era on Woodward and Campus Martius. **Manning Brothers Historical Collection.**
CENTER: Looking south on Woodward from Grand Circus Park. **Schramm collection. LOWER:** Woodward and the
Boulevard area. **Schramm collection.**

Ford's Highland Park plant across from the D.U.R. main shops. **Faber Collection.**

Ave. Cars carrying "Woodward-Elizabeth" wyed at Elizabeth Street and Woodward Ave. at the north edge of the business district. Cars going to 3rd. Street and West Jefferson Ave. had the destination signs of "Woodward-Through". Northbound cars carried the regular Woodward route but the destination sign of "Limits" wyed at Woodward and Cortland Avenues. Those with "House" signs turned at the Woodward Car House. "Log Cabin" cars looped at Log Cabin Park, and during the State Fair day all carried "Fair Grounds" signs.

The Elizabeth wye came into being in an interesting manner. In the early morning rush hours most of the northbound passenger traffic originated north of Adams Street, which meant that southbound Woodward cars ran empty to their destination. Since a turning spot was desirable somewhere north of Witherell to save this dead mileage, a wye was needed. The city would not permit the D.U.R. to lay tracks on side streets. So in the summer of 1915 the National Elks Lodge was to hold their national convention in Detroit and planned a parade on Woodward from Adams. The D.U.R. was able to obtain a permit for a "temporary" wye at Elizabeth Street to permit the turning of the cars during the parade. The city granted the request, and then both the city and D.U.R. forgot about the temporary nature of the wye.

Another odd piece of track was off the northbound track on Woodward at Campus Martius. This spur track held about four cars and was used to transport people home after downtown theaters were closed. There were usually Pontiac Division interurbans there to take people home to Royal Oak, Birmingham

and Bloomfield Center. Another spur for car storage ran off the southbound track on the north side of Amsterdam to Cass Ave. This spur was used to store cars in the afternoons - ready to pick up passengers from the Cadillac, Studebaker, Regal and other automobile firms and industrial plans in this section.

A four track yard existed at Battery K, at Woodward and Cortland Ave. where "Limits" cars turned. The main classification yard for the Woodward-Pontiac Division was at the Fair Grounds. Cars were picked up by Construction cars at Gratiot and Mt. Elliott yards where they had been loaded with automobile bodies from Clay Ave. and Piquette yards and together with general merchandise from the Electric Depot at 5th. and Congress streets were transferred in the early evening to the Fair Grounds. At this point, electric locomotives took over for the Pontiac and Flint haul.

One of the heavy transfer points was at Warren where the Crosstown crossed Woodward, the reason was that no other crosstown line existed, which meant a person going from Highland Park to the Dodge Plant in Hamtramck had to take a Woodward car, then the Crosstown car and then a Baker Car. This required two transfers as the Crosstown was a three cent line having a light transfer with dark lettering. The Baker and Woodward were five cent lines with transfers printed on brown paper with black lettering. On the Woodward line, one asked the conductor for "one of each" if you wanted a Crosstown-Baker transfer. If you intended to ride two three cents lines you asked for "two of a kind".

The wealthy people lived along Woodward in 1916 — and we imagine that was the reason the roadbed was so well maintained and the cars dept in as quiet operating condition as possible. Many of the residents were stockholders in the company which was a "blue chip" stock selling (when available) at $115 per share. The cars operated were 1375 to 1499, with four motors double truck type, and all equipped to pull trailers. The trailers were single truck with interchangeable bodies. In the winter they were the closed 600 Ponchar-trains, and during the summer open bodies of the 700 and 800 series. In the later part of 1916 the 5000 series trailers were placed in service, followed by the 3000 series steel cars.

The Woodward line was a standard D.U.R. line Storage air was taken on at Battery K and Woodward Car House, and the Michigan-Depot cars at 14th. and Marquette pumping station.

Woodward south of the Log Cabin when it was still open country. **Faber Collection.**

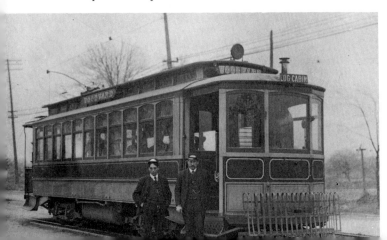

TOP: The Norris line on-again-off-again service faced another interruption in service in 1915. A car barn fire destroyed the two cars which resulted in service being halted temporarily. Meanwhile, new track work at the railroad crossing on Jos. Campau was designed to eliminate the need for an isolated route and car barn. By 1917 the line was back in service. The Davison line extended east to connect with the Norris line but it did not last. By 1918 the city was reaching out along its route. Car 1533 is on Jos. Campau at Bismarck. **BOTTOM:** Grand Belt cars, loading on Clark at Fort in 1919. Factory shift change times placed many cars on the line besides the normal service. These extra cars called trippers usually made a single trip per shift. **Both Manning Brothers Historical Collection.**

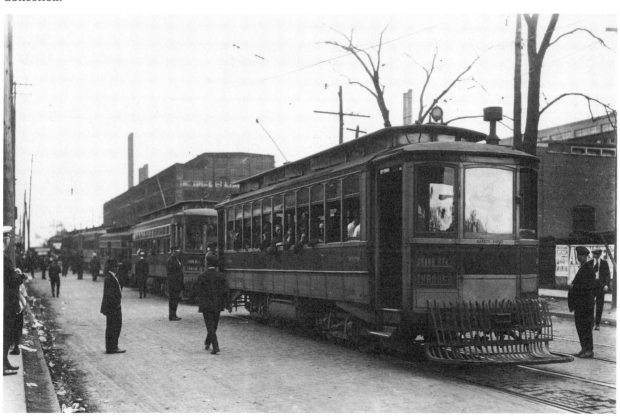

TOP: The Myrtle line built in 1886 operated horsecars till late 1896, when it was electrified. This line served a sparsely populated area as seen by this posed photograph. Yet, today, the area is within the inner city. **Burton Historical Collection, Detroit Public Library. BELOW:** By the time car 1270 arrived, the area was already under heavy development. **Clarence Woodard Collection.**

Chapter 4—Municipal Operation

THE CITY BUILDS A COMPETING SYSTEM

Between the defeat in 1919 of the proposal to purchase the D.U.R. and the final take over in 1922, is another period in which Detroit again had more than one company operating streetcars in the city. The City of Detroit, operated streetcars on their own lines in competition with the D.U.R. This system was referred to as the Municipal Operation (M.O); therefore, we have used this term to separate it from the period after the entire D.U.R. system was taken over by the City of Detroit.

A dominate figure of the period was James Couzens, a self made man of hard work, leadership, and a flair for business. Jim, as his friends called him, left Canada to accept a job in Detroit as a freight checker for the Michigan Central Railroad. His quick business sense brought him into contact with the Ford Motor Company. First he was Ford's business manager, later General Manager of the Corporation. While serving as a D.S.R. Commissioner from July 7, 1913, until February 2, 1916, he became a strong advocate of Municipal Operation of the city streetcar system and began to consider himself an expert on transportation.

Couzens decided he would become Mayor of Detroit with a political platform that advocated the take over of the D.U.R. For publicity in 1918, when the D.U.R. had raised fares one cent, he arranged to be removed from a streetcar for refusing to pay the new fare. The newspapers were on hand to give it full coverage. Jim Couzen's campaign was successful; he became Mayor of Detroit in April of 1919. Couzens renewed his determination to compel the D.U.R. to sell to the city.

Detroit needed a rapid transit system to relieve downtown congestion but financing it was the problem. The second Barclay, Parson's and Klapp survey recommending a rapid transit system was submitted to the D.S.R. Commission which in turn submitted it to the Common Council on October 22, 1919. The formation of a new company was recommended using the existing D.U.R. operations as a base and adding 92.0 miles of much needed extensions and new equipment. To cover the cost, the city would issue $20,000,000 in bonds to obtain the needed funds at a low rate of interest. The city would control the fares and financing, and would be able to purchase the entire operation at any time. In the meantime profits were to be used to build a subway. Their study of Detroits traffic problems resulted in their recommending the building of downtown subways with surface or elevated rail further out as the only solution. The plan was called "Detroit-Service-at-Cost-Plan".

The Mayor was against the plan, instead he now favored reactivating a plan to build a competing system. In early 1919, prior to reaching agreement on the price offered to D.U.R., the Council had proposed a $10,000,000 bond issue to begin construction of a piece-meal system. The D.S.R. Commission favored the subway plan, therefore, having opinions conflicting with the Mayor on the subject and being political appointees of the Mayor, they resigned en-masse on November 9, 1919. The Council was divided on the issue but passed a resolution to begin negotations with the D.U.R. to put this plan into operation. This ordinance was vetoed by the Mayor, and the Council's attempt to override the veto failed by one vote. Thus, by this narrow margin Detroit lost not only rapid transit which still has not been built, but a peaceful solution to its transportation problems.

On January 20, 1920, the Castator Ordinance was presented and until the vote on April 5, 1920, a lively campaign was waged. The City's (or Couzens) sale pitch included a motto, "Service-at-Once". Even a professional motion picture was prepared for showing at the neighborhood theaters to obtain the voter's backing. Newspapers gave daily listings of where it could be seen. There were almost daily editorials, letters, articles, and cartoons which were anti-D.U.R. appearing in the papers.

The proposals were to sell $15,000,000 in bonds to pay for the following:

1. The city would take over the track on Woodward from the River to Milwaukee, also on Fort from Artillery to Baldwin, as the franchise on this track had expired. It was planned to pay $850,000 for this 21.25 miles of track.
2. The total trackage built under the "Day to Day Agreements", which amounted to 29.48 miles to be purchased for $1,370,000.
3. The City would begin immediately to build 100.25 miles of new track at a estimated cost of $70,000 per mile.
4. The City would purchase 400 cars at $10,000 each and 150 trailers at $5,000 each, a total of $4,750,000.
5. To spend $1,000,000 for barns, tools and miscellaneous equipment.

The D.U.R. countered with a "Service-at-Cost-Plan" similar to Clevelands; however the City Attorney ruled their proposal failed to meet certain legal requirements. The D.U.R. appealed to the Circuit Court which ordered the City Attorney to place the plan on the ballot. This was not done by Mr. Wilcox, the City Attorney. Later he was appointed D.S.R.'s General Counsel by Mayor Couzens.

On April 5, 1920, the citizens voted Mayor Couzens the funds to build the municipal system. Within 24 hours the Mayor appeared before the press turning a shovel full of dirt to inaugurate "Big Jim's City Streetcar System".

On February 1, 1921, the first operation began on the St. Jean line with 6 cars, and also on Charlevoix (this line was also called Crosstown by the M.O.) with 10 cars giving 5 minute service. The fare was five cents with a free transfer good only between the two M.O. lines. By the end of 1921, the M.O. was operating on 52.6 miles of track they had built.

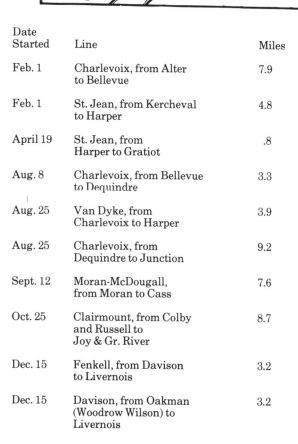

Plan for Proposed Municipal Street Railway System
For full description of the red lines and numbers read the other side

FINANCIAL PLAN FOR "A" & "B" LINES

Present trackage to be taken over at cost less depreciation as specified at the
time company was given permission by city to build under a Day-to-Day
agreement:

34.25 miles estimated at $40,000.	$1,370,000.00
Fort and Woodward tracks where franchise has expired 21.25 miles estimated at $40,000.	850,000.00
New tracks in unserved districts, 100.75 miles estimated at $70,000.	7,052,500.00
400 new electric motor cars estimated at $10,000 each.	4,000,000.00
150 new trailers estimated at $5,000 each.	750,000.00
(If the Ford gas car is used, the cost of cars will be reduced about 50 per cent.)	
Car Barns, tools, etc.	1,000,000.00
Total	15,022,500.00

This $15,000,000.00 bond issue is for 30 years and will be paid by yearly
installments through that period.

The Class "C" lines, consisting of 62 miles, will be developed as soon as "A"
and "B" are in operation.

The $15,000,000.00 bond issue covers the building, equipping and where
it is proposed, the taking over, of a total of 156 miles of the complete system of 218 miles.

KEY

Present D. U. R. System,	—— Black Lines
D.U.R. Lines Taken Over, Nos. 11 to 21, Inclusive	
New City Owned System,	■ Red Lines
City Limits	
Boulevards	

Date Started	Line	Miles
Feb. 1	Charlevoix, from Alter to Bellevue	7.9
Feb. 1	St. Jean, from Kercheval to Harper	4.8
April 19	St. Jean, from Harper to Gratiot	.8
Aug. 8	Charlevoix, from Bellevue to Dequindre	3.3
Aug. 25	Van Dyke, from Charlevoix to Harper	3.9
Aug. 25	Charlevoix, from Dequindre to Junction	9.2
Sept. 12	Moran-McDougall, from Moran to Cass	7.6
Oct. 25	Clairmount, from Colby and Russell to Joy & Gr. River	8.7
Dec. 15	Fenkell, from Davison to Livernois	3.2
Dec. 15	Davison, from Oakman (Woodrow Wilson) to Livernois	3.2

JAMES J. COUZENS

ADJACENT PAGE: Mayor "Big Jim" Couzens driving the first spike on August 23, 1920 on Harper Avenue. **D.S.R. Files.**

Mayor Couzens had promised to build 100 miles of track. But, by February 18, 1921, when construction began on the Van Dyke line, the system was still short of its goal of 100 miles. At the time a slogan, "A-Mile-A-Day" appeared on the Departments vehicles. Neither goal was realized.

The total trackage operated by the M.O. was listed the 1924 arbitration.

Built	61.48 miles
Purchased (Harper)	.92 miles
	62.40

To state that Mayor Couzens fell short of his promises is obvious. To mitigate his inability to produce the promised system and to get the voters attention in the 1922 election, he went forward with a plan to eliminate the D.U. R. completely from the streets.

During 1921, the city was still putting pressure on the D.U.R. to relinquish its tracks into downtown. The M.O. found that without access to the city center they were unable to compete. Therefore, to accomplish this the city decided to take over all trackage built under the "Day to Day Grants" given the D.U.R. after 1911. They contained portions of the heavy traveled lines such as Grand Belt, Hamilton, Mack and Third.

On April 4, 1921, the voters again approved the purchase of the "Day to Day" trackage. The M.O. and D.U.R. entered arbitration over the tracks value.

How involved the valuation became is exemplified in the Hamilton line trackage. First in 1911, a temporary line was authorized. It was built in 1912 and put into operation in February 1913. The D.U.R. contended it was temporary construction built on "an improved country road (dirt) newly brought into the city" and the line was built to provide service until final construction could be completed. The city contended it was original trackage and on April 3, 1913, the grade of the street was established by the city. The D.U.R. now was forced to begin reconstruction in July 1913, of a new permanent, center of the road track which would now replace the side of road track had to be born by the D.U.R. and none of the cost could be recovered in the sale of the line to the city, since the arbitrators felt it was now non-existant property.

The D.U.R. countered that the 128 cars and trailers used on this Day-to-Day trackage must also be purchased by the M.O. since they would no longer be needed. Agreement was reached and on December 23, 1921, the city took over the track and 105 cars that included numbers 3021-3125 and 23 trailers, 5100-5122. The agreed price was $2,297,277. Also included in the agreement was a provision that the D.U.R. could continue using any needed track but pay a rental of $.20 per car mile.

On July 8, 1921, the agenda of the D.S.R. Commission contained two important items. First, the ordering of the first 50 Peter Witt style streetcars from the Kuhlman Company. These double truck cars were the forerunner of a fleet totaling 781 cars which became the backbone of Detroit's streetcar service. These cars were a vast improvement over 250 single truck Birney's with which the city attempted to provide service. The Mayor later stated he had allowed these cars (Peter Witts) to be ordered in a weak moment and was not in favor of their use in place of the Birney's.

The second item on the agenda was a meeting with the D.U.R. to set a price on the Fort Street and Woodward Avenue trackage. On July 14, 1921, a letter setting an offer of $338,000 was sent to the D.U.R. which felt this was about scrap value.

Then on November 8, 1921, the people voted for an ordinance to force the D.U.R. to remove their tracks wherever their franchises had expired. This was the club which Couzens used to end D.U.R.'s city operations.

The D.U.R. faced with the loss of Woodward and Fort and the use of trackage under the "Day-to-Day" agreements, agreed to mutual running rights on the following lines;

Line	Date Joint Service Began
Trumbull, from Davison & Oakman to Larned & Shelby	12-15-21
Woodward, from Jefferson to Palmer Loop (Six Mile)	1-2-22
Hamilton, from Palmer (Six Mile Road) to Atwater & Woodward	1-2-22
Fort-West, from Woodward via Fort to Dearborn Wye	1-16-22
Fort-West, from Woodward via West Jefferson to River Rouge	1-16-22
Fort-East, from Woodward to Baldwin	1-16-22

The agreement covered the following trackage:

D.U.R. tracks	69.1 miles
M.O. tracks	36.0 miles
Day to Day tracks	29.5 miles

The Grand Belt and 14th lines were also included, however, the D.U.R. continued to operate these lines through lease of the tracks. The rentals were $.20 per car mile by either party, and the cars were stored at the D.U.R. car houses for $5.00 per day. Schedules were jointly made for the lines with the D.U.R. operating the odd numbered runs and the M.O. the even numbered runs. The men on the board, who held these runs had selected them by line seniority, either stayed with the D.U.R. or transferred over the M.O. on this basis.

The fares on all M.O. lines were quickly increased by charging $.01 for a transfer, with the D.U.R. and M.O. splitting fares even. The city that had so long advocated the three cent fare was unable to operate for one year on a five cent fare with a free transfer. The D.U.R. had been forced to operate the Pingree lines until 1919 with the three cent fare. Even with this fare increase, the M.O. was unable to make the money promised by Mayor Couzens.

On January 6, 1922, negotiations to allow the city to lease the entire one fare trackage in the city on a day-to-day basis as a preliminary step to the city purchasing the D.U.R. system, was turned down by the D.U.R. due to the companys financial condition. The city then informed the D.U.R. that if they did not come to the next D.S.R. Commission meeting with a price satisfactory to the city, they would enforce the ouster ordinance approved November 8, 1921. The D.U.R., on January 12th, offered to sell, for $25,000,000, all remaining property in the one fare

zone in Detroit. This bid did not include the Day-to-Day property already sold making a total price of $27,797,277. This price was for the same property for which, in 1919, the city had agreed to pay $31,500,000. To this offer Mayor Couzens stated he would not pay over $20,000,000. The ouster ordinance was not enforced due to a request of Mr. Gringra, who stated he represented 70,000 shares of D.U.R. stock and that at the next stockholders meeting of February 7, 1922, there would be a reorganization of the D.U.R.

At the annual stockholders meeting February 7, there was a change in management of the D.U.R. with a new group ready to sell out for whatever they could salvage from the city operation. The Mayor, holding one share, attended and delivered a message from the city in which he reviewed the past battles and how the D.U.R.'s fight to stay in operation (and not give it all away for scrap value) had forced the city into expensive court fights which increased the bonding interest rates. By this time the city would offer no more than $16,500,00. However, by March 13, agreement was reached on a figure of $19,850,000 for the remaining property within the one fare zone. The agreement provided for a down payment of $2,770,000 semi-annual payments of $500,000 plus 6% interest.

On April 7, 1922, the voters approved the purchase with a $4,000,000 bond issue to cover the down payment and balance to cover needed material costs. Much of this was to cover debts of the M.O. operations since the city operations were never profitable.

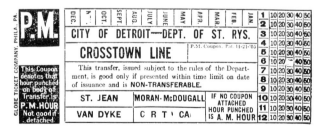

To Our Patrons==

This is your Street Railway and that we may operate it to your greatest satisfaction we seek your advice and co-operation.

We respectfully request that you submit suggestions and criticisms at all times. These will be given prompt consideration.

Communications should be addressed
Board of St. Railway Commissioners, City Hall

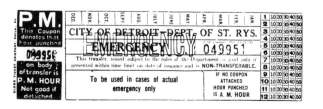

Three tokens were introduced on August 20, 1921. Two were the size of nickels, one indicated 5¢ fare, and the other was good for a fare without any amount indicated. The other token was the size of a dime. On September 2, 1923 the sale of tokens was discontinued; they ceased being good for fares on January 20, 1924. **LEFT:** Three transfers from the M.O. operation. **ABOVE:** The backs of the transfers were used for promotional purposes.

TOP AND ABOVE: Two Birneys were passing each other on Cass north of Davenport. Below car 168 with a "Crosstown" sign turning off Elliott onto John R. The M.O. called this the Crosstown line even issuing transfers with that name(see previous page). **BOTTOM:** The M.O. portion of the Trumbull line. At this time the M.O. and D.U.R. were jointly operating this line; the M.O. was using the large Peter Witts Car 11032 had originally been numbered 1032 but had been renumbered due to confusion with D.U.R. cars. **Manning Brothers Collection.**

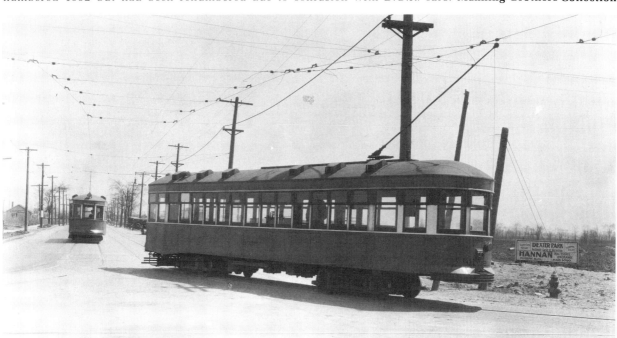

OPERATING THE SYSTEM

On April 6, 1920, the day following the favorable vote, the first shovel full of dirt was turned signalling the beginning of construction of Detroit's City-owned system. Mayor Couzens drove the first spike on August 23rd. Even with this fast start, by October 1, 1920 the city cancelled their contracts with private builders and hired Mr. H.P. Hevenour to take charge. He changed the type of track construction from the D.U.R. standard type to what was called monolithic type construction. This was to reduce the cost and speed up construction.

The M.O. had no rail work cars even after they took over their own construction. All material was hauled by truck or horse and wagon. The material removed from the streets to make a base for the tracks, was hauled to Belle Isle to enlarge the island. This was Detroit's only lasting benefit from this operation.

From December 15, 1920, to January 15, 1921, all departments were concentrating on the inauguration of service which had been ordered by City Hall to take place by February 1, 1921. By January 15, the electrical department had completed approximately ¾ of their work in welding the tracks, setting poles, and stringing wire on the St. Jean and Charlevoix lines.

Back in mid-November 1920, the M.O. had adopted a color scheme for their cars; yellow body, maroon and white stripping, black running gear, and all cars lettered, "City of Detroit-Department of Street Railways".

On January 5, the first car arrived, and by the 15th there were 20 cars on the property. These cars turned out to be little single truck Birney Safety Cars, not the promised large cars with trailers needed to haul the large crowds. These cars were such a failure that by 1924 the D.S.R. was attempting to sell 200 of the 250 purchased, at a fraction of their cost. This was the second largest fleet of Birneys gathered in the nation. The D.S.R. was able to sell 56 of these cars, and by 1930 half of the remaining cars were not usable. The rough ride and crowd handling capacity of these small cars might be compared to the subcompact automobiles, fitted with hard springs and wooden seats.

On January 16, 1921, the electrical power from Detroit Edison was applied to the overhead at Waterloo and St. Jean. General Manager Goodwin was at the controls as car #100 became the first car to operate.

To store these cars, land had been purchased in an area bounded by Shoemaker, Lillibridge, Warren and St. Jean Streets, on Detroit's east side, and by January 31st a temporary car house was built. On May 15, 1922, this was replaced by a permanent car house and the headquarters for the D.S.R. were located on this site. The headquarters remained here until 1972 when they, and the main repair shops in Highland Park were moved to a more central location. The shops were the last piece of D.U.R. property owned by the D.S.R.

The streetcar situation, its poor tracks, and overhead wire created reams of copy for the press.

Hostile news stories appeared almost daily. The papers took the position that the D.U.R. could do no right and the city could do no wrong. Big Jim had the D.U.R.'s days numbered. Even in the last hours the D.U.R. tried to fight back but its leaders were aging. Therefore, the M.O. continued to wrap its rails around and over the D.U.R. An example of the city's attempt to break the D.U.R. at any cost is evident in how and where their lines were constructed. CHARLEVOIX - BUCHANAN (CROSSTOWN) - There had been a need for years for a crosstown line which did not go through the congested downtown area. One route proposed by the D.U.R. had been the linking of Mack and Myrtle, but approval was never given. The M.O. decided to parallel this route and the existing D.U.R. trackage using Charlevoix on the east side, and Buchanan on the west side, and connecting them through many narrow streets. Charlevoix itself was so narrow in some areas that after laying the double track and widening the street at city expense, the light poles ended up in the center of the sidewalks. Other streets such as Eliot, which had been a tree shaded, 26' residential street, became after the addition of a double track and widening, a 40' treeless traffic congested street. The residents who objected were quickly over-ruled in the courts.

This line was called Crosstown for many years, even though the D.U.R. had a line operating with the same name on Warren and Forest. The line began operating on February 1st, to Bellevue where a crossover was installed for the cars to return. Then during 1921, the line was pushed to completion using two seven-hour shifts, and on August 25, 1921, the line was operating to Junction. The service was provided by small Birney cars, on a six minute headway on the base and three minute headway during rush hours. It took 58 minutes to cross the city with a two minute layover. One newspaper at the time noted it crossed 25 railroad tracks at grade, 13 at one point.

Transferring lines were St. Jean which by April 19th was operating from Gratiot to Charlevoix. On August 25th the Van Dyke line from Harper to Charlevoix, and on Sept. 3, the Moran-Mc Dougall began. This line started at Milwaukee & Moran to Palmer, to Mc Dougall, to Mack, then used the Charlevoix tracks across Woodward to Cass. This duplication of service was soon discontinued as the M.O. found the cost of operating streetcars was more then the revenues received and was forced to reduce service. St. JEAN - On May 6, 1920, the Council revoked the day to day franchise given the D.U.R. to build the St. Jean line on May 27, 1919, even though work had began. The D.U.R. had installed the base, track and ties, on Harper from Montclair to Gratiot, also had begun excavating on St. Jean between Waterloo and Kercheval. The Council also recinded the resolution ordering the Rapid Railway (Leesville Line) to replace their single track on the north side of Harper from Gratiot to Van Dyke with a double track in the center of the street.

The city sent the Police Superintendent and the Superintendent of the Public Works to stop work on the St. Jean line, threatening to arrest the supervisors if they failed to order their men to stop work. Then

Detroit's first Birney being unloaded on St. Jean north of Shoemaker on a temporary siding. **BELOW:** A line up of Birneys on Shoemaker probably going to the training track on Montclair between Harper and Shoemaker. **D.S.R. Files.**

after completing the M.O. line to Harper, the city ordered the D.U.R. on February 1st, to remove all their tracks and material, from Montclair to Gratiot on Harper. The D.U.R. went to court asking damages and the city was ordered to pay $50,000. Using the D.U.R. tracks, the M.O. was soon able to extend the St. Jean line to Gratiot.

The St. Jean line was also famous for the crossing fight at St. Jean and Mack where the line crossed the D.U.R. tracks. Knowing that the D.U.R. would fight the crossing the M.O. decided to do it in the middle of the night. The date was January 9, 1921, shortly after mid-night. D.P.W. workmen were instructed to report to the eastern yard at 9:00 p.m. Saturday, but were not told why. The D.P.W. workmen were loaded in trucks at 12:15 a.m. for the trip to St. Jean and Mack. There the D.U.R. had parked a large truck over the intersection, two blocks away were two large snow plows parked. The D.P.W. men moved the large truck from the crossing and before the snow plow could

arrive, they dumped 12 loads of crushed stone blocking them. By 10:00 a.m. the first city car had crossed the intersection.

D.U.R. General Manager Burdick had become suspicious and went to a Circuit Court Judge's home to obtain a restraining order which would be good even on Sunday. During the commotion, Mr. Burdick attempted to have the writ served, but was arrested and sent to Belle Isle. Here the city figured the D.U.R. lawyers would have difficulty in locating him because the Belle Isle bridge was then a swing bridge, and would be closed at night. It was later rebuilt as a non-operating bridge. Mr. Burdick and John Kerwin (D.U.R. Superintendent of ways and structures) who had accompanied him, were rescued by boat as related by Mr. Kerwin's nephew. In later years Mr. L.R. Wagner who after 40 years, retired as head of Engineering for the D.S.R., often related how one of his first jobs was driving a team of horses over the crossing to prove its safety.

143

TOP: A survey photo of the site purchased by the M.O. bounded by Warren, St. Jean, Shoemaker, and Lillibridge. The farm house beyond the barn was, in later years, to become a restaurant for D.S.R. employees. The barn and hothouses were soon gone after this 1921 photo. **CENTER:** The M.O. hurriedly installed temporary tracks to park their large fleet of 250 Birneys and 50 Peter Witts.

RIGHT: Car 119 in front of the temporary car house used during early M.O. days. **D.S.R. Files**

144

TOP: Mayor Couzens was quoted as stating he allowed 50 Peter Witts to be ordered in a weak moment. On October 8, 1921 the first cars arrived under their own power from from Cleveland taking 12 hours for the trip. They used the Lake Shore Electric Railway and D.U.R. interurban track. The cars travelled only during the day light hours since they were not equipped with powerful enough headlights for night travel. Car 1020 sits in front of the temporary car house on November 14, 1921.

CENTER: The M.O. had no property connected to the railroad; therefore, they built a temporary siding on St. Jean north of Shoemaker, and another north of Shoemaker where the Federal-Mogual plant was built in 1942. This was called Candler Yard and rail cars brought in the gravel needed for the roadbed. Here the fleet of trucks used to haul it were loaded. **D.S.R. Files.**

The next two pages have a series of track construction pictures showing the monolithic type track construction adopted by the M.O. to speed up the laying of track and reduce cost. The D.U.R. type construction required a trench twenty-two inches deep; then eight inches of cement; one inch of sand on which was laid the track and wooden ties; then it was filled to grade with cement. The monolithic type construction only required a trench seventeen and one-half inches deep; a two inch slag base was laid; the track with steel ties; then it was filled to grade with crushed Wisconsin granite which was rolled and refilled to grade with grout and rolled again.

The concrete was prepared in a central mixing plant. It was hauled up to 1000 feet in either direction by a narrow gauge side dumping railway using a kerosene engine pulling up to five cars. There were three sets of cars for each engine. **D.S.R. Files.**

1 - Breaker 211 on McDougall between Superior and Willis.
2 - Steam shovel 212 on McDougall south of Warren.
3 - Laying rails at Moran & Boulevard Ct.
4 - Rails and steel ties on Seldon near Greenwood.
5 - Straightening rails at Mack & Dubois.
6 - Track welders on Mack east of Chene.
7 - Special work at Warren & St. Jean.
8 - Laying concrete at Elmwood & Charlevoix.
9 - Trains at the Boulevard & McGraw.
10 - Laying concrete at Arndt & McDougall.
11 - Clearing tracks on Van Dyke south of Moffat.
12 - Spreading crushed stone on Eliott east of John R.
13 - Rolling crushed stone on Van Dyke north of Mack.
14 - Grouting machine at Gratiot and Van Dyke.
15 - Grouting machine on Van Dyke north of Warren.
16 - Grouting machine at Harper & Monclair, note Birney at what was then end of St. Jean line.

ABOVE: Woodward car with Michigan Central and Grand Trunk Railway crossing in background. **D.U.R. Files.**
BELOW: Starting January 22, 1922, the D.U.R. and the M.O. operated joint service on Woodward Avenue. (Other routes were, also, joint operations) A new overhead traffic control signal was being installed and tested as M.O. car 3110 passes two inbound D.U.R. cars. In twenty days the M.O. would be operating all city lines under the name D.S.R. **Tom Dworman Collection. ADJACENT PAGE:** Fort Street in 1921 from First Street looking toward cars on Third Street. On the left beyond the steeple is the Union Station. On the right (light colored building) is the Detroit News which also housed the studio and transmitter of WWJ which began broadcasting September 1, 1920. **D.U.R. Files.**

CLAIRMOUNT LINE - On October 25, 1921, the second crosstown line began operating from Grand River & Joy to Linwood, to Clairmount, to Owen, to Russell, to Colby (near Grand Blvd.) Up to this time the operations had been confined to a single car house on the east side. Now a temporary car storage yard called Joy Road Car station located at Woodmere and Joy was opened. The Clairmount line was extended January 30, 1922 over tracks taken from the D.U.R. Grand Belt line from Buchanan to Grand River, via 35th, Junction, Epworth, and Joy Road. On the east side on Milwaukee from Russell to Moran, then using the M.O. Moran-Mc Dougall tracks to Van Dyke. The M.O., after being undecided which route to use in connecting the Clairmount line to Charlevoix on the east side, decided to use Van Dyke. On February 13th, the line was extended. This resulted in Moran-Mc Dougall becoming a "plug" line. The Van Dyke line was in later years replaced by the St. Jean line as the eastern portion of the Clairmount line and never became a major route.

The D.U.R. found itself being pushed to the wall. Each time they planned to give service to the population of Detroit, the city would stop them and then tell the press that D.U.R. does nothing for the people. By 1921, Mayor Couzens took the next step in his determined plan to destroy the D.U.R., he forced the joint operation of key lines and interchange of transfers (the transfer exchange ceased immediately after the D.U.R. takeover).

On December 15, 1921 the M.O. began operating the Trumball line jointly with the D.U.R. and began service on Davison between Oakman (Woodrow Wilson) and Livernois. This line was known as the West Davison line. The route operated jointly from downtown to Oakman & Livernois, from there the D.U.R. cars continued on their regular route to the Woodward Car House, north of Manchester. The city cars continued on new trackage (sometimes referred to as the Fenkell line) to Livernois and Fenkell. The M.O. used Peter Witts on Trumball, and Birneys on Davison, all cars for both lines used the D.U.R. carhouses paying $5.00 per day per car.

By agreement the M. O. took over one half of the men on the Trumbull Board, the manner used was that the M.O. took over all the odd numbered employees and the even numbered remained with D.U.R. In later years when the city took over the lines, they were combined and the operators retained their original seniority date on the line.

Then on January 22, 1922 joint service began on Woodward from the Log Cabin (Palmer Park north of Six Mile Road) to Third and Jefferson. The depot portion of this line was continued as a separate line by the D.U.R. To meet car requirements, the D.U.R. lent the M.O. 20 trailers numbered 5205-5224, and the city lent the D.U.R. 20 of the cars recently purchased from them, numbered 3045-3064.

On the same day joint service began on the Hamilton line from Woodward & Atwater to Hamilton & Six Mile Road. The last lines operated jointly were on Fort on January 16th, when East Fort from Baldwin & Lafayette to Congress & Bates began with both companies using Birney safety cars. The West Fort line began from the West Jefferson Car House to Larned & Shelby, also Fort & Dearborn (Woodmere Division) to Larned & Shelby. The trackage west of Dearborn remained a D.U.R. line called, Miller Road. The cars used on West Fort were either the double truck cars purchased from the D.U.R., or Peter Witts.

The following two pages have eight photos of the Charlevoix-Buchanan line taken during 1921.

1 - The eastern terminus Alter Road and Charlevoix.
2 - In front of Liberty Motors (Budd) Company.
3 - Note the narrow street used for double tracks at Van Dyke and Charlevoix.
4 - After completion power and telephone poles ended up in the center of sidewalks on Charlevoix just east of Crane.
5 - Passing East Grand Boulevard with the cement light poles.
6 - Crossing the Michigan Central tracks between Bellvue and Beaufeit.
7 - Taken August 21, 1921, the first day of operation between Sheldon west of Cass.
8 - Working on the Michigan Central and Grand Trunk Railroad crossings at Buchanan and Tillman.

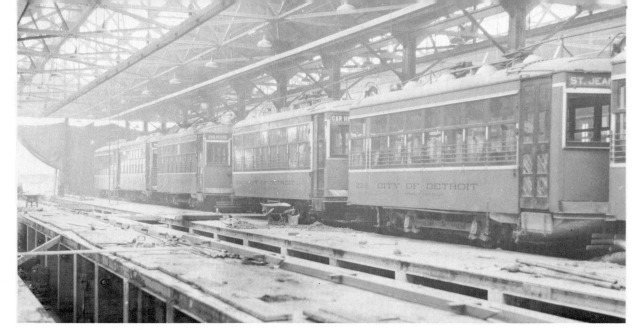

UPPER: Birneys in the new car house which replaced the temporary car house. Note that the doors were not installed yet. **D.S.R. files.** **CENTER:** Installing the overhead at Harper and Montclair. Since the M.O. had no work cars this wagon was used until line trucks were purchased later in the year. **Schramm collection. BOTTOM:** Birney 185 crossing Woodward at Davenport, on August 21. 1921, **D.S.R. files.**

Chapter 5 — Epilogue

The final day of a private enterprise street railway company in Detroit was quickly approaching. Under the leadership of Hazen Pingree, the city first attempted to convert the city transit system into municipal ownership. This attempt almost succeeded but the time was not right. It had to await a change in the social attitude of the city.

Shortly after World War I, government control of many public services had become a reality. With a big push from "Big Jim" Couzens, the city's mayor, it became acceptable for a city such as Detroit to own its transit system. The people voted to back the mayor in his drive to have the city assume control of the D.U.R.'s city lines. The result would be the then largest municipal system in the country. On the morning of May 15, 1922, the Department of Street Railways operated all street railway service within the city limits. Municipalization was achieved.

TOP: An M.O. Birney on the over built shuttle line at Palmer and Beaufait. Note the tower and signal system. **D.S.R. file. CENTER:** D.U.R. car passes Hazen Pingree's statue in Grand Circus Park in the waning years of the D.U.R. city service. **Manning Brothers Historical Collection. LEFT:** Fort line joint service. Deck roof D.U.R. car precedes M.O. car 1044 on West Jefferson loop. **Thomas Dworman Collection. NEXT PAGE:** Map of the street railway system at the time of total municipalization on May 15, 1922.

DETROIT, MICHIGAN

STREETCAR TRACKAGE AT MAY 15, 1922

—————— Trackage of the Detroit United
Railway

- - - - - - Trackage built by Municipal
Operation

+—+—+ Interurban Trackage

PRW = Private Right-of-way
C. H. = Car House

Mile Scale

0   1/4   1/2   3/4   1

MAZ

State Fair Grounds

Lesure Av.

Extension of Woodward Av.

A—A

Grand River Av.

Oakman Hwy.

Turner Av.

Utica Av.

Ewald Circle

Ewald Circle

Livernois Av.

Livernois Av.

Fenkell Av.

Oakman Hwy.

Davison Av.

12th St.

Woodrow Wilson

PRW

Elmhurst Av. PRW.

PRW.

Webb Av.

Hamilton Blvd.

Palmer P. Loop

Six Mile Road

City Limits

Woodwa C.H.

PRW

Battery
Cortland

Dailey Av.

Highfield

Mackinaw Av.

Joy Rd.

Grand River Av.

Linwood Av.

12th St.

Clairmount Av.

Pingkee A

Epworth Blvd.

Casper Av.

Livernois Av.

Addison Av.

Michigan Av.

Devereaux St.

35th St.

Junction Av.

31st St.

McGraw Av.

Warren Av.

Ferry Park Av.

Holden Av.

Lincoln Av.

Milwau

Baltimo
Amsterda C.H.

14th Av.

Trumbull C.H.

Trumbull

Third Av. C.H.

Greenwood Av.

Third Av.

Holden Av.

Warren C.H.

Warren Av.

Forest Av.

Buchanan St.

Canfield Av.

Lincoln Av.

Roosevelt Av.

24th St.

18th St.

12th St.

Selden Av.

Myrtle St.

Davenport St.
Stimson Av.

Temple Av.

Henry St.

Michigan C.H.

Junction Av.

Livernois Av.

Toledo Av.

Dix Av.

24th St.
23rd St.

Dalzelle St.
M.C. Depot

15th St.

Marantette Av.

Brooklyn Av.

(See Deta

Ford Motor Co.

Tractor Av.

PRW

Industrial Av.

Dix Av.

Ferndale Ave.

Woodmere Av.

Springwells Av.

Chamberlain St.

Baker C.H.

Dragoon C.H.

Scotten Av.

24th St.

Baker St.

Porter St.

Howard St.

Abbott St.

5th St.

W. Fort St.

Congress St.

Jefferson Av.

Interurban
Freight Terminal

D.M. & T.
Interurban Terminal

Dearborn Av.

Boyd St.

Clark C.H.

Clark Av.

W. Jefferson Av.

Fort C.H.

Detroit River

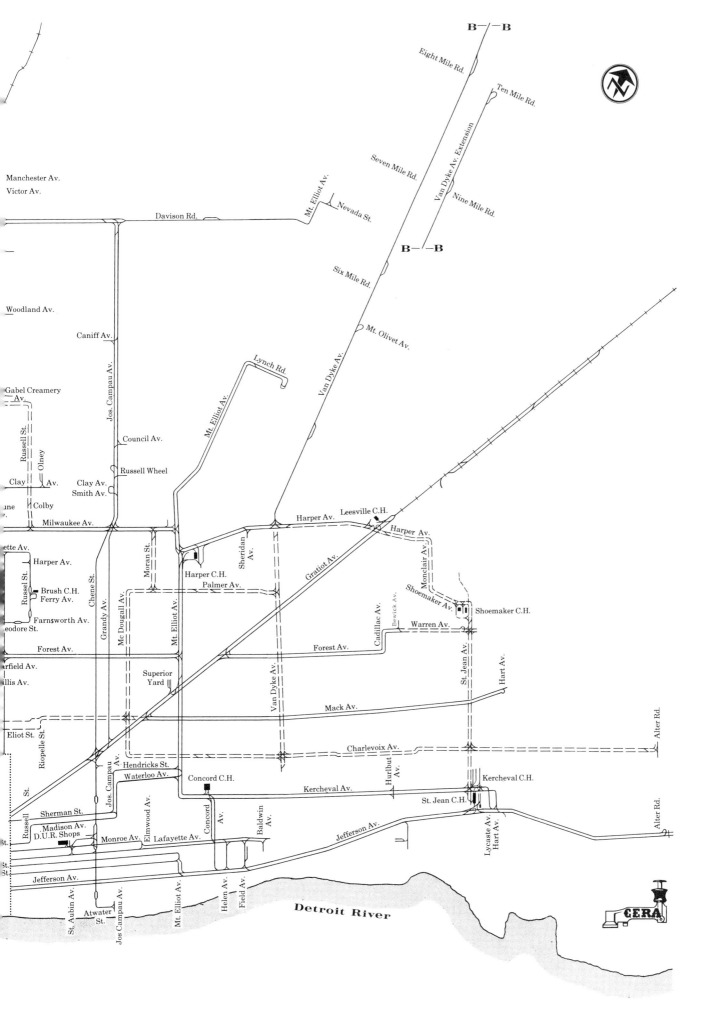

B—B

Eight Mile Rd.

Ten Mile Rd.

Van Dyke Av. Extension

Seven Mile Rd.

Nine Mile Rd.

Manchester Av.
Victor Av.

Davison Rd.

Mt. Elliot Av.

Nevada St.

B—B

Six Mile Rd.

Woodland Av.

Caniff Av.

Mt. Olivet Av.

Jos. Campau Av.

Gabel Creamery
Av.

Lynch Rd.

Russell St.
Olney

Council Av.

Clay
Av.

Clay Av.
Smith Av.

Russell Wheel

Mt. Elliot Av.

Van Dyke Av.

une

Colby

Milwaukee Av.

Harper Av.

Leesville C.H.

Harper Av.

ette Av.

Harper Av.

Moran St.

Sheridan
Av.

Monclair Av.

Shoemaker Av.

Russel St.

Brush C.H.
Ferry Av.

Chene St.

Harper C.H.

Palmer Av.

Gratiot Av.

Shoemaker C.H.

eodore St.

Farnsworth Av.

Grandy Av.

Mc Dougall Av.

Mt. Elliot Av.

Cadillac Av.

Bewick Av.

Warren Av.

St. Jean Av.

Hart Av.

Forest Av.

Forest Av.

arfield Av.

llis Av.

Superior
Yard

Van Dyke Av.

Mack Av.

Alter Rd.

Eliot St.

Riopelle St.

Charlevoix Av.

Hurlbut
Av.

Jos. Campau
Av.

Hendricks St.

Kercheval C.H.

Waterloo Av.

Concord C.H.

Kercheval Av.

Russell
St.

Sherman St.

Madison Av.
D.U.R. Shops

Monroe Av.

Elmwood Av.

Lafayette Av.

Concord
Av.

Baldwin
Av.

St. Jean C.H.

Jefferson Av.

Lycaste Av.
Hart Av.

Alter Rd.

St.

St.

Jefferson Av.

St. Aubin Av.

Atwater
St.

Jos Campau Av.

Mt. Elliot Av.

Helen Av.

Field Av.

Detroit River

CERA

© CERA 1978

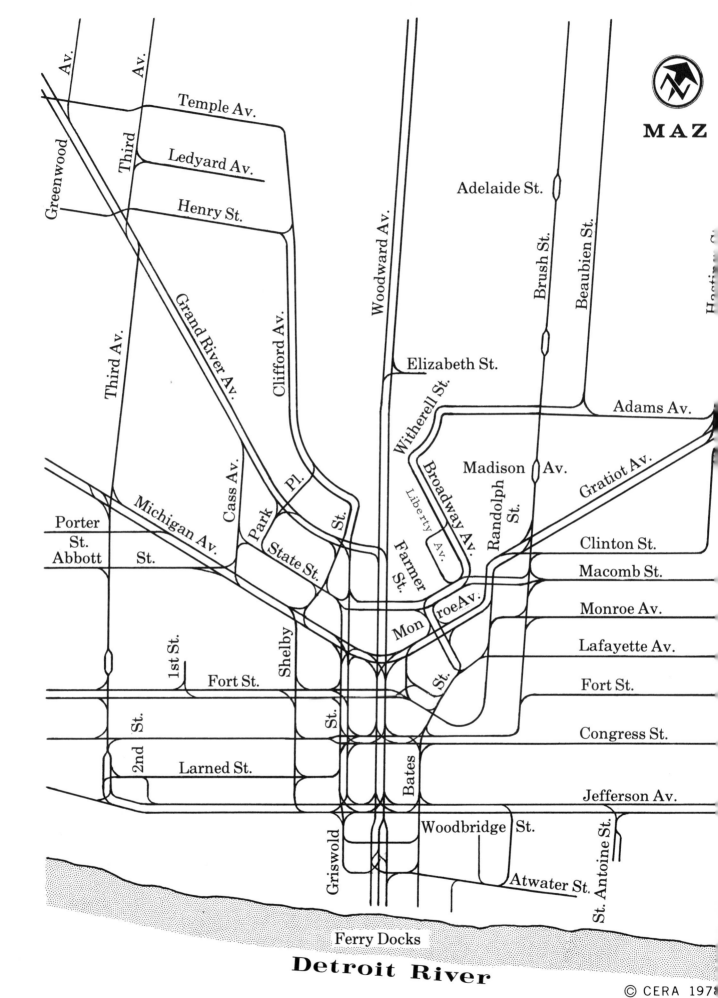

MAZ

Temple Av.

Ledyard Av.

Henry St.

Adelaide St.

Greenwood

Third

Third Av.

Grand River Av.

Clifford Av.

Woodward Av.

Brush St.

Beaubien St.

Elizabeth St.

Adams Av.

Witherell St.

Madison Av.

Gratiot Av.

Broadway Av.

Cass Av.

Pl.

Randolph St.

Clinton St.

Porter St.

Michigan Av.

Park

St.

Liberty Av.

Macomb St.

Abbott St.

State St.

Farmer St.

Monroe Av.

1st St.

Shelby

Mon roe Av.

Lafayette Av.

Fort St.

St.

St.

Fort St.

2nd St.

Congress St.

Larned St.

Bates

Jefferson Av.

Griswold

Woodbridge St.

St. Antoine St.

Atwater St.

Ferry Docks

Detroit River

© CERA 1978

CENTRAL BUSINESS DISTRICT

CORPORATE HERITAGE — DEPARTMENT OF STREET RAILWAYS

GRAND RIVER STREET RAILWAY
Grant May 1, 1868
Reorganized January 17, 1890

GRAND RIVER RAILWAY CO.
Sold October 1, 1891

DETROIT CITIZENS STREET RAILWAY COMPANY
Incorporated August 31, 1891
Merged December 31, 1900

DETROIT, FORT WAYNE & BELLE ISLE RAILWAY COMPANY
Incorporated March 1, 1898
Merged December 31, 1900

DETROIT UNITED RAILWAY INCORPORATED

DEPARTMENT OF STREET RAILWAYS
Commenced operations May 15, 1922

CENTRAL MARKET, CASS AVE. AND THIRD STREET RAILWAY CO.
Incorporated May 31, 1873
Reorganized August 23, 1877

CASS AVENUE RAILWAY CO.
Merged June 22, 1882

DETROIT STREET RAILWAY CO.
Sold September 16, 1891

DETROIT, RIVER ROUGE AND DEARBORN STREET RAILWAY CO.
Incorporated June 14, 1889
Sold June 5, 1893

FORT WAYNE & BELLE ISLE RAILWAY COMPANY
Incorporated May 23, 1892
Sold April 1, 1898

DETROIT SUBURBAN RAILWAY COMPANY
Merged December 31, 1900

DETROIT & FLINT RWY.
Incorporated August 10, 1901
Merged August 1, 1901

MUNICIPAL OPERATIONS
Opening Day - February 1, 1921

DETROIT & GRAND JUNCTION RAILWAY COMPANY
Grant June 13, 1873
Reorganized September 17, 1875

CONGRESS & BAKER STREET RAILWAY COMPANY
Merged June 22, 1882

DETROIT CITY RAILWAYS CO.   Incorporated May 12, 1863
Reorganized December 1, 1890

HAMTRAMCK STREET RAILWAY
Incorporated May 1, 1869
Merged November 1, 1881

FORT STREET & ELMWOOD RAILWAY CO.
Grant January 31, 1865. Name changed in 1871 to FORT WAYNE AND ELMWOOD RAILWAY COMPANY
Reorganized July 1, 1892

DETROIT RAILWAY, Incorporated December 10, 1894. Reorganized July 29, 1896 as DETROIT ELECTRIC RAILWAY. Merged December 31, 1900

JEFFERSON AVENUE RAILWAY COMPANY
Grant March 13, 1881
Merged November 1, 1892

HIGHLAND PARK RAILWAY
Incorporated May 12, 1886
Merged February 1, 1893

DETROIT ELECTRIC RAILWAY COMPANY
(Dix Avenue Railway) Grant April 17, 1886
Merged November 1, 1892

GRATIOT AVENUE RAILWAY CO.
Grant May 7, 1891
Merged November 1, 1892

DETROIT, UTICA & ROMEO RWY.
Incorporated August 10, 1898,
Sold September 4, 1901

NORTH DETROIT ELECTRIC RWY.
Incorporated August 8, 1899
Sold October 10, 1901

DETROIT & LAKE ORION RWY.
Incorporated March 22, 1899. Name changed on June 3, 1899 to DETROIT, ROCHESTER, ROMEO & LAKE ORION RWY. Name changed on November 28, 1899 to DETROIT, LAKE ORION & FLINT RWY., Sold August 28, 1901

Excluded from the chart are:
St. Aubin Street Railway (1873-1876) Tracks removed
North Detroit & Chene (1891-1892) Tracks removed
East Detroit & Grosse Point (1887-1892) Tracks removed

157

Chapter 6 — Rosters of Equipment

HORSE CARS

Few records of the horse-car era equipment survive. Thus, we are unable to provide a complete list of equipment used in that era. However, a list of cars in service on September 16, 1891, the last horsecar roster, survives and it is representative of the number and types of vehicles utilized.

Type	Builder	Purchased	Number
Detroit City Railway			
Double	Jones	1882	2
Double	Jones	1883	6
Double	Jones	1885	16
Double	Brill	1885	8
Double	Ontario Car Co.	1885	8
Double	Jones	1886	4
Double	Pullman	1886	10
Double	Jones	1887	26
Double	Brill	1888	2
Double	Jones	1888	15
Double	Jones	1889	18
Double	Brill	1889	10
Double	Lewis & Fowler	1889	20
Double	Jones	1890	16
Open	Jones	1888	38
Open	Brill	1888	30
Double	Eaton	Very old	9
Single	Various	1880-2	30
Flat	D.C.R. Co.	1891	2
		Subtotal	280
Grand River Railway Co.			
Double	Unknown	1869	2
Double	Brill	no date	7
Double	Brill	1888	2
Double	Lewis & Fowler	1889	11
Double	Brill	1889	10
Open	Lewis & Fowler	1889	10
Single	Pur. from D.C.R.	1890-1	4
		Subtotal	46
		Grand total	326

Notes
1) Double: A car that requires two horses.
2) Single: A car that uses one horse, usually nicknamed a "bobtail".
3) Number of horses required:

Detroit City Railway	1,572
Grand River Railway	377
	1,949

ELECTRIC STREETCARS PURCHASED PRIOR TO 1922

Company records of the early Detroit streetcars are no longer available due to time and fire. To present this roster, the following sources were used:

M.E. Cooley, 1899 survey of Detroit streetcars, located at the University of Michigan, Transportation Library, Ann Arbor, Michigan.

Clarence Faber material from the Burton Historical Collection in the Detroit Public Library. Additional material from the Faber Collection made available by Clarence Woodard.

The 1909 Barcroft Appraisal of the D.U.R. properties prepared for the City of Detroit.

The 1919 survey of D.U.R. equipment prepared for the proposed purchase of the D.U.R.

Files of the Department of Street Railways regarding the M.O. (Municipal Operations).

All rosters are in numerical order. D.U.R. data includes all cars purchased, taken over from predecessor companies, or built by the D.U.R. Numbers are D.U.R. assigned numbers. Earlier numbers, if known, are indicated. M.O. data includes all cars purchased during this short period of competing service. We grouped similar cars with a few selected photos to assist in identification and listed the assigned group number under photo group on the roster.

DETROIT UNITED RAILWAY
Early Electrics-Closed Cars

Car Number	Builder	Lot No.	Date Delv.	Trucks	Motors	Control	Weight	Seats	Length Body	Length Overall	Width	Notes	Photo Group
42-44	Well & French			S-Brill 21	2-W 12	Steel D	18,800	21	18'0"	27'0"	7'6"	From Detroit & North-western Rlwy.	—
51-75	D.U.R.		1901	S-Dupont	2-Steel-29	W K-12	24,340	29	22'8"	34'9"	8'0"	Later #77-79 Double ended	6
76-79	Brill	4418	1892	S-Brill	2-Steel D	Steel D	19,160	34	21'0"	31'10"	7'7"		2
87-98 or 86-97	Jones		1892	S-Dupont	2-Steel D	Steel D		21	16'0"	24'2"	7'5"	Original equip Detroit Electric Works.	1
101	Detroit Cit. Rly.		1897	S-Dupont	2-West 49	West 28	26,400	29	24'8"	36'8"	8'6"	Original "Yolande" later put in regular service	(a)
102-175	St. Louis		1895	S-Brill 21	2-W 12a	W K-12	24,700	30	22'8"	31'6"	9'4"	Originally #2-75. #1 was rebuilt as funeral car.	3
176	D.U.R.		1901	S-Dupont	2-Steel 29	W K-12	24,340	29	22'8"	34'9"	8'0"		6
177-203	Kuhlman		1896	S-Dupont	2-W 12a	W K-12	24,640	30	22'6"	30'10"	9'3"	Originally #77-103	3
204-242	D.U.R.		1901	S-Dupont	2-Steel 29	W K-12	24,340	29	22'8"	34'9"	8'0"		6
243-246	Brill			S-Brill 21	2-Steel D	Steel D		21	18'0"	27'0"	8'0"	Original Flint City cars, all double ended	—
247-271	D.U.R.		1901	S-Dupont	2-Steel 29	W K-12	24,340	29	22'8"	34'9"	8'0"	Original #9-14 from Wyandotte Div.	6
272-277	Jackson &Sharp			S-Dupont	2-Steel D	Steel D	20,500	25	21'0"	32'7"	7'7"		—

Ex-Horsecars-Closed Cars

Car Number	Builder	Lot No.	Date Delv.	Trucks	Motors	Control	Weight	Seats	Length Body	Length Overall	Width	Notes	Photo Group
278-279	Brill		1895	S-Dupont	2-Steel D	Steel D		25	21'6"	29'8"			5
280	Jones		1895	S-Dupont	2-Steel D	Steel D	20,300	25	22'3"	31'3"	7'0"		5
281-286	Lewis & Fowler		1895	S-Dupont	2-Steel D	Steel D	20,180	25	21'2"	30'1"	7'6"		5
287-293	Jones		1895	S-Dupont	2-Steel D	Steel D	20,300	25	22'3"	31'3"	7'0"		5
294-295	Lewis & Fowler		1895	S-Dupont	2-Steel D	Steel D	20,180	25	21'2"	30'1"	7'6"		5
296-299	Jones		1895	S-Dupont	2-Steel D	Steel D	20,300	25	22'3"	31'3"	7'0"		5

Early Electrics-Closed Cars

Car Number	Builder	Lot No.	Date Delv.	Trucks	Motors	Control	Weight	Seats	Length Body	Length Overall	Width	Notes	Photo Group
300	D.U.R.		1901	S-Dupont	2-Steel D	Steel D	24,340	29	22'8"	34'9"	8'0"		6
301-385	Stephenson		1895	S-Dupont	2-Steel D	Steel D	20,800	26	22'0"	31'2"	7'6"		1
386-391	Brill	6627	1895	S-Brill	2-Steel D	Steel D		34	20'0"	30'8"	7'7"		2
392-400	D.U.R.		1901	S-Dupont	2-Steel D	Steel D	24,340	29	22'8"	34'9"	8'0"		6
401-420	Pullman	758	1892	S-Dupont	2-Steel D	Steel D	20,460	23	20'0"	29'2"	7'6"	Originally #298-317, equipped by Detroit Electric Works	1
421-425	Pullman	763	1893	S-Dupont	2-Steel D	Steel D	20,460	23	20'0"	29'2"	7'6"	Originally #318-322, equipped by Detroit Electric Works	1

159

Car Number	Builder	Lot No.	Date Delv.	Trucks	Motors	Control	Weight	Seats	Length Body	Length Overall	Width	Notes	Photo Group
426-435	Pullman	775	1893	S-Dupont	2-Steel D	Steel D	20,460	23	20'0"	29'2"	7'6"	Originally #328-339, equipped by Detroit Electric Works	1
436-440	Brownell		1893	S-Dupont	2-Steel D	Steel D		23	20'0"	30'8"	7'7"	Originally #323-327	1
441-455	Stephenson		1895	S-Dupont	2-W 12	Steel D	22,000	25	20'2"	31'5"	7'7"	Originally #41-55	1
Ex-Horsecars-Closed Cars													
456-457	Burned at Baker Car House 1895 — no information available												—
458-461	Jones		1895	S-Dupont	2-Steel D	Steel D	20,300	25	22'3"	31'3"	7'0"		5
462-467	Lewis & Fowler		1895	S-Dupont	2-Steel D	Steel D	20,180	25	21'2"	30'1"	7'6"		5
468-472	Brill		1895	S-Dupont	2-Steel D	Steel D		25	21'6"	29'8"			5
473	Jones		1895	S-Dupont	2-Steel D	Steel D	20,300	25	22'3"	31'3"	7'0"		5
474-478	Brill		1895	S-Dupont	2-Steel D	Steel D		25	21'6"	29'8"			5
479	Jones		1895	S-Dupont	2-Steel D	Steel D	20,300	25	22'3"	31'3"	7'0"		5
480-483	Lewis & Fowler		1895	S-Dupont	2-Steel D	Steel D	20,180	25	21'2"	30'1"	7'6"		5
484-493	Jones		1895	S-Dupont	2-Steel D	Steel D	20,300	25	22'3"	31'3"	7'0"		5
494-495	Brill		1895	S-Dupont	2-Steel D	Steel D		25	21'6"	29'8"			5
496-499	Jones		1895	S-Dupont	2-Steel D	Steel D	20,300	25	22'3"	31'3"	7'0"		5
Early Electrics-Open Bench Cars													
501-550	Stephenson		1895	S-Dupont	2-Steel D	Steel D		48	20'4"	28'4"	7'0"	Later some Double ended	4
553-572	Pullman	776	1893	S-Dupont	2-Steel D	Steel D		45	23'3"	30'6"		Originally #340-370	4
573-600	Pullman	777	1893	S-Dupont	2-Steel D	Steel D		45	23'3"	30'6"		Originally #371-387	4
601-700	Stephenson			S-Dupont	2-Steel D	Steel D	21,100	50	25'0"	32'6"	7'0"	Many rebuilt as closed cars, seat 31, also as trailers in later years	4
701-738	Jones			S-Dupont	2-Steel D	Steel D		50	25'9"	33'4"	6'9"	May have been old horse cars.	4
739-769	Brill			S-Dupont	2-Steel D	Steel D		50	26'3"	33'9"	6'11"		4
770-779	St. Louis			S-Dupont	2-Steel D	Steel D		50	25'10"	33'2"	7'2"		4
780-785	Brill	6429	1895	S-Dupont	2-Steel D	Steel D		50	21'0"	31'3"	7'6"		4
786-810	Detroit Cit. Rly.		1900	S-Dupont	2-Steel D	Steel D		60	27'4"	34'6"		Many used as trailers in later years	4
811-825	D.U.R.		1901	S.Dupont	2-Steel D	Steel D		60	27'4"	34'6"	7'6"	Many used as trailers in later years	4
Double Truck-Cars													
826-845	Stephenson		1902	D-St. L	4-W 12a	W K-6		70	34'0"	42'1"		Original Wyandotte open bench suburban cars	7

Car Numbers	Builder	Sample Car	Year	Truck	Motor	Control	Weight	Seats	Length (body)	Length (overall)	Width	Notes	Ref
826-845	Rebuilt Kuhlman	476, 483-4	1911	D-St. L	4-W 12a	W K-35	42,850	42		46'8"			7
Single Truck-Cars													
850-899	Cincinnati	1730	1913	S-Dupont	2-GE 203		28,750	28	23'2"	34'7"	8'3"		12
900-999	American	962/972	1912	S-Dupont	2-W 68	W K-11	27,700	28	23'2"	34'7"	8'2"		12
1002-1025	D.U.R.		1901	S-Dupont	2-W 49	W K-12	24,260	29	22'8"	34'9"	8'0"		6
Double Truck-Cars													
1026	D.U.R.		1901	D-Brill 27	4-W 56	W K-14		53	40'5"	51'4"	8'6"	Second "Yolande" #7004 rebuilt as funeral car and renumbered	(b)
1027	Det Citizen Ry		1902	D-Dupont	4-Steel 34	W L-4		38	33'1"	44'4"			(b)
1028-1052	St. Louis		1903	D-Brill 27f	2-GE 57	W K-12	37,300	36	28'0"	40'8"	8'3"	First double truck city cars	8
1053-1102	St. Louis	367	1903	D-Brill 27f	2-GE 57	W K-12	37,300	40	29'0"	41'4"	8'3"	Cars #1138-1152 built by American #520 for Brill	9
1103-1152	Brill	13128	1904	D-Brill 27f	2-W 56	W K-12	37,300	40	29'0"	41'4"	8'3"		9
1153-1177	Brill	568	1905	D-Brill 27f	2-W 56	W K-12	37,300	40	29'0"	41'4"	8'3"	Built by American for Brill	9
1178-1202	St. Louis	489	1905	D-St. L 47	2-W 56	W K-12	37,300	40	29'0"	41'4"	8'3"		9
1203-1227	Kuhlman	403	1909	D-St. L 47	2-W 93a	W K-12	40,000	40	29'0"	41'4"	8'6"		9
Single Truck-Cars													
1250-1261	D.U.R.		1905	S-Dupont	2-W 38	W K-12	28,420	30	23'0"	34'9"	8'3"	Cross seat cars with side aisles	10
1262-1273	D.U.R.		1906	S-Dupont	2-W 38b	W K-12	28,420	30	23'0"	34'9"	8'3"	Cross seat cars with side aisles	10
1274-1299	Cincinnati	505	1906	S-Dupont	2-W 93a	W K-12	28,420	30	23'0"	34'9"		Cross seat cars with side aisles	11
1300-1329	Cincinnati	655	1906	S-Dupont	2-W 93a	W K-12	28,420	30	23'0"	34'9"	8'6"	Cross seat cars with side aisles	11
Double Truck-Cars													
1375-1424	Kuhlman	548	1913	D-Std 050	4-GE 203	W K-35	*47,350	45	31'4"	44'0"	8'6"		14
1425-1474	Kuhlman	548	1913	D-Std 050	4-GE 203	W K-35	*47,100	45	31'4"	44'0"	8'4"		14
1475-1524	Kuhlman	526	1912	D-Std 050	2-GE 210	W K-35	43,000	45	31'4"	44'0"	8'6"		14
1525-1574	Kuhlman	511	1911	D-Std 050	2-GE 210	W K-35	43,000	45	31'4"	44'0"	8'6"		14
1575-1609	Kuhlman	481	1911	D-Brill 27e	2-GE 210	W K-35	44,400	45	31'4"	44'0"	8'7"		14
Double Truck-Cars													
1610-1624	Niles		1911	D-Std 050	2-GE 210	W K-35	44,400	45	31'3"	44'2"	8'7"		14
1625-1649	Niles	463	1910	D-Std 050	2-W 310	W K-35	41,800	43	31'2"	42'2"	8'5"		13
1650-1699	Kuhlman	449	1910	D-Std 050	2-W 310	W K-35	41,600	43	31'4"	42'2"	8'8"		13
1700-1749	Cincinnati	795	1907	D-Std 050	2-W 93a	W K-35	37,800	40	29'0"	41'4"			9
1750-1774	Cincinnati	1180	1910	D-Std 050	2-W 310	W K-35	41,000	43	31'3"	42'3"	8'4"		13

Roster table — streetcar equipment

Car Number	Builder	Lot No.	Date Delv.	Trucks	Motors	Control	Weight	Seats	Length Body	Length Overall	Width	Notes	Photo Group
1775–1799	Kuhlman	432	1909	D-Brill 27	2-W 310	W K-35	42,650	43	31'3"	42'3"	8'4"		13
Double Truck-Steel Body Cars													
3000-3005	Kuhlman	608	1915	D-Std 050	4-GE 203	W K-35	46,400	46	33'6"	46'10"	8'4"		15
3006-3024	Kuhlman	608	1915	D-Std 050	4-GE 203	W K-35	47,140	46	33'6"	46'10"	8'4"	#3019 heated by oil	15
3025-3049	Kuhlman	616	1916	D-Std 050	4-GE 203	W K-35	47,140	46	33'6"	46'10"	8'4"		15
3050-3099	Kuhlman	636/637	1917	D-Std 050	4-GE 203	W K-35	47,140	46	33'6"	46'10"	8'4"		15
3100	D.U.R.		1918	D-Std 050	4-GE 203	W K-35	47,140	46	33'6"	46'10"	8'4"	First arch roof city cars	15
3101-3125	D.U.R.		1919	D-Std 050	4-GE 203	W K-35	47,140	46	33'6"	46'10"	8'4"	Similar to #3101-3125	15
3126-3146 Retained by the D.U.R. for Flint city and suburban service.													
Trailers													
5000-5049	Kuhlman	609/610	1915	D-Brill AB	———	———	26,800	52		46'9"	8'4"		16
5050-5099	Kuhlman	614/615	1916	D-Brill AB	———	———	26,800	52		46'9"	8'4"		16
5100-5149	Kuhlman	619/620	1916	D-Brill 67f	———	———	26,800	52		46'9"	8'4"		16
5150-5199	Kuhlman	638/639	1917	D-Brill l 67f	———	———	27,260	52		46'9"	8'4"		16
5200-5249	D.U.R.		1920	D-D.U.R.	———	———	28,000	52		46'9"	8'4"		16
MUNICIPAL OPERATIONS									*Length*	*Width*	*Height*		
Birney Safety Cars													
100-124	Osgood Bradley	6400	1921	S-O.B. 25-96	2-GE 264	K36BR	16,000	32	28'0"	7'10"	10'10"		17
125-149	Osgood Bradley	6520	1921	S-O.B. 25-96	2-W 508A	K36BR	16,800	32	28'0"	7'10"	10'10"		17
150-249	Brill	21316	1921	S-Br 79	2-W 508A	K36BR	17,360	32	28'0"	7'10"	10'8"	Some had 2-GE-264 motors	17
250-274	McGuire Cumming		1921		2-W 508A	K36BR	16,000	32	28'1"	7'11"	10'0"		17
275-324	St. Louis	1258	1921	S-St. L	2-W 508A	K36BR	16,000	32	28'0"	8'3"	9'10"		17
325-349	Osgood Bradley	6590	1921	S-O.B. 25-96	2-GE 264A	K36BR	16,000	32	27'10"	7'10"	10'10"	Some had 2-W 508A motors	17
Peter Witts													
1000-1049	Kuhlman	751		D-Brill 77El	4-GE 265	K-35	37,320	52	48'6"	8'6"	10'10"	Renumbered #11000-11049, later #3200-3249	18

Cars and trailers received 12/23/21 from the D.U.R. as part of Day to Day Purchase

3021-3125	Motor cars see D.U.R. section for data												15
5100-5122	Trailers see D.U.R. section for data												16

GROUP 1 — EARLY ELECTRICS — CITIZENS RAILWAY

In 1892 when the Citizens decided to change over to electrical operation on Jefferson Avenue they used small 16' car bodies which could be used either with electrical motors or horse power. The bodies were furnished by the J.M. Jones' Sons Company of West Troy, New York (1864-1912). The motive equipment came from the Detroit Electric Works. These early cars still retained the open front and rear platforms.

Soon as additional lines were electrified, larger cars were ordered from Pullman Company, Chicago, Illinois, Brownell Car Company, St. Louis, Missouri (1857-1902) and John Stephenson Car Company, New York City (1830-1904). By the end of the 1890's the motor cars usually were equipped with Steel "D" motors and DuPont single trucks. Also, the front platform was enclosed to protect the motorman. This was a result of union pressure and city ordinances.

The Citizens Railway had in its employ a talented engineer, A.B. DuPont. He was responsible for a streetcar truck design appearing on many transit systems including Detroit, St. Louis, Louisville, and Cleveland. Also, DuPont is credited with the design of the Detroit style platform.

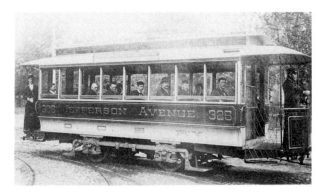

UPPER: The Citizens first electrics used on Jefferson in 1892. There are no known photos showing their original appearance. This 1923 photo shows car 93 which had been rebuilt in 1897 into the D.U.R. pay car. The original open platform had been enclosed.

CENTER: The third builder to furnish cars was Brownell. Five cars were purchased in 1893 for the Jefferson line. Originally numbered 323-327; later renumbered 436-440. By 1909 they were all double ended. The last car 438, which had been in Flint, ended up as a shelter on the Stephenson line 12/28/21.

BOTTOM: These cars built by Stephenson for Brooklyn but diverted to Detroit became the first electrics on Grand River. Originally numbered 41-55, they had long carpet covered seats on each side. These 23 seat cars were electrically heated and lighted. By 1919, all these cars were converted to one man operation. **D.U.R. files.**

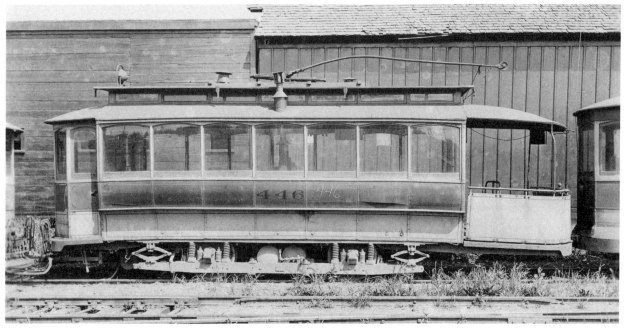

ABOVE: This 1893 photo shows the second group of cars purchased and includes the first 20 car used on Woodward. These Pullman built cars were first numbered 298-317, 318-322 and 328-339 later renumbered 401-435 (two cars had been removed from service).**Schramm Collection.**

Two photos of the Pullman cars in later years with their front platform enclosed. Many of these cars after service in Detroit were transfered to the smaller cities such as Flint as larger cars were required in Detroit. Photo at left was taken in 1915 as new Highland Park Shops were under construction. **Faber Collection.**

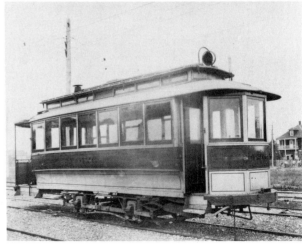

The largest order of early electrics went to the Stephenson Company in 1895 for 85 cars with the front platform enclosed. These cars were placed in service on the major lines, and until the turn of the century, were the backbone of the fleet. They seated 28 on their longitudinal seats.

UPPER: shows original appearance of cars. **CENTER:** front end shot of car 338. **BELOW:** Picture taken October 7, 1897 showing car 353 passing car 367 on Woodward as the Detroit Opera House was burning. **First two D.U.R. files the last from the Burton Historical Collection.**

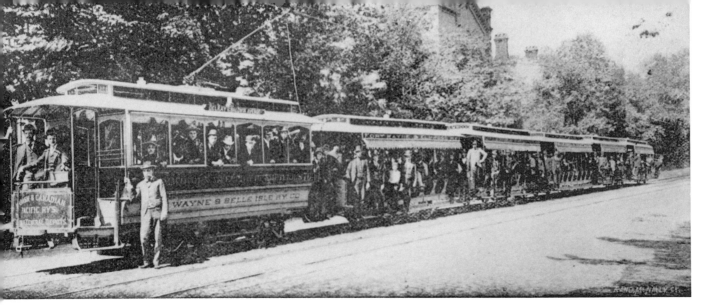

GROUP 2 — EARLY ELECTRICS — FORT WAYNE AND BELLE ISLE RAILWAY

This company converted to electricity on its single line shortly after the Citizens Company did on Jefferson Avenue. There is little information available on the company's cars. The Street Railway Journal in 1892-4 listed 57 horsecars prior to electrification and 57 trailers after, which would indicate no horsecars were converted to electrics.

Two purchases of electric closed cars were recorded; first, in 1892 for 30 eighteen-foot cars; and again, in 1895 for 6 twenty-foot cars. Both purchases were from Brill in additon to six open bench cars. The original numbers of the first order is not recorded. Only the latter car numbers have been recorded in inventories ranging from 49 through 82 with company records noting 78 as the first electric to operate on their line. One reason for this lack of information was that after the take over by the Citizens Railway, Tom Johnson stated all the Fort Wayne cars remaininng in service were to be rebuilt with the larger Detroit platform.

The second order of electrics by 1899 were numbered 386-391 and the open bench cars 780-785.

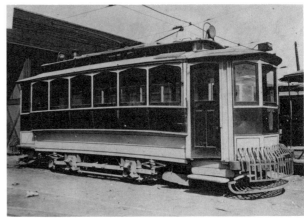

TOP: Car 78 pulling a string of trailers on West Fort Street. **Faber Collection. CENTER:** Car 78 rebuilt into a double ended car with both platforms enclosed and enlarged. **Faber Collection. BOTTOM:** Car 76 waiting to be scrapped. Note the small platform on the cars. **D.U.R. Files.**

GROUP 3 — EARLY ELECTRICS — DETROIT RAILWAY

The Detroit Railway was built as a electric system, accordingly, all their cars were electric. These cars were considered one of the best of the early electric convertibles having removable sides. Yet, photos of any cars in service with the sides removed have not been found. By the turn of the century the running boards on aisle side had been removed. These cars were fast and carried a good load, and were used to service the three cent Pingree lines. In 1912 these cars were replaced by new single truckers numbered 850-999 because they could not be used for "pay-enter operation adopted by the D.U.R. Mr. Lloyd Judge in his notes, to the authors, who worked for the D.U.R. noted "I remember playing in a large line of side door 102-175 class cars on the scrap line-trucks and motors removed, but equipment still aboard. These were along the south side of the Highland Park barns. A few weeks later we went back to play but found only piles of ash and old iron".

These cars were built on what was referred to as the "Kuhlman Pattern" having cross seats, a side aisle, and three doors on the aisle side. The cars had on the back of each seat a push button connected with a battery and a bell on the rear platform so the passenger could signal the conductor to stop. The center door was controlled from the rear platform. Each car was equipped with two fare boxes; one for fares, and one for tickets.

ABOVE: The first order for 76 cars went to the St. Louis Car Company in 1895. These cars seated 30 on their painted seats with spindal backs and rattan cushions. This company photo of their first car shows the original lettering and were numbered 1-76 later renumbered 102-175. Car 1 was rebuilt into a funeral car by 1897. One car was out of service by the time of renumbering. **Henning Collection.**

BELOW: A rear view of car 1 showing the box like construction of these wide cars. These cars were the widest of the early electrics in Detroit. **Dworman Collection.**

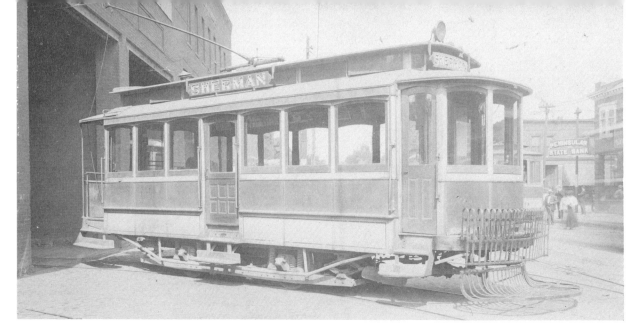

TOP: Car 132 still serving the 3¢ lines, now painted in D.U.R. colors, waiting in front of Concord House at Concord and Kercheval. Today, this location is a playfield. Note the running board has been replaced by steps. **Faber Collection. MIDDLE AND BOTTOM:** The Detroit Railway's second order was for 27 cars and went to the Kuhlman Company. Numbered originally 77-103, they were renumbered 177-203. Here are two street photos of car 181 after renumbering and using a stove replacing the original electric heaters. **Faber Collection.**

GROUP 4 — THE OPEN BENCH SUMMER CARS (ALL COMPANIES)

The numbers of these cars were from 550 through 825. The builders included Stephenson, Pullman, Jones, Brill St. Louis and the Citizens and Detroit United Railway. The cars through 785 were 10 bench, while the last series 786-825 were the larger 12 bench. As with the early horse cars, many of these cars in later years were used as trailers. The city made their use in the city illegal in 1918. Many of the 600 series were rebuilt into closed cars or trailers.

TOP: Builders photo of Stephenson open bench car taken at company's shops in 1895. Note the striped curtains and lack of headlights. Later, lights were installed on the roofs. This series of cars were numbered 501-550. **Burton Historical Collection. MIDDLE:** Car 533 in service. **Faber Collection. BOTTOM:** A Fort Wayne and Belle Isle Company open bench car built by Brill. The original numbers are unknown, except the photo in the chapter on electrification includes a car from this group numbered 41. These cars also originally had no headlights. **Faber Collection.**

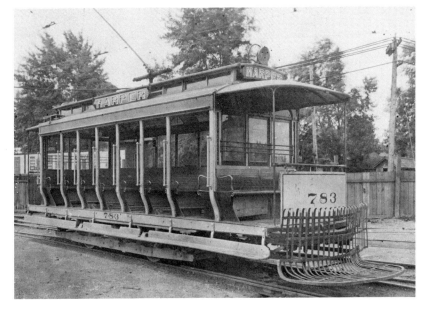

169

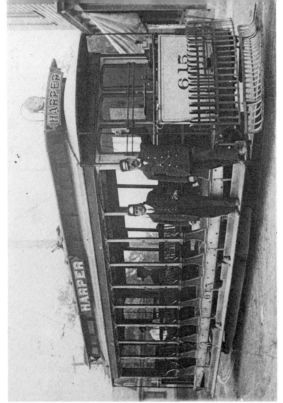

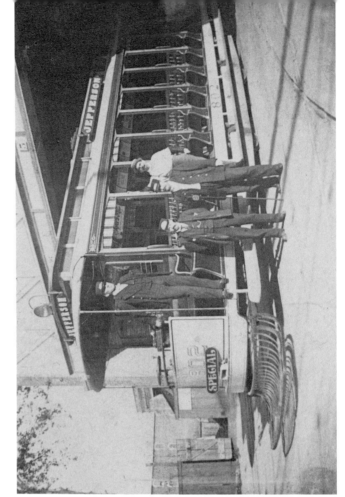

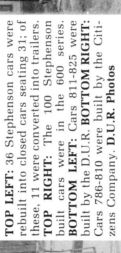

TOP LEFT: 36 Stephenson cars were rebuilt into closed cars seating 31; of these, 11 were converted into trailers. **TOP RIGHT:** The 100 Stephenson built cars were in the 600 series. **BOTTOM LEFT:** Cars 811-825 were built by the D.U.R. **BOTTOM RIGHT:** Cars 786-810 were built by the Citizens Company. **D.U.R. Photos**

GROUP 5 — EX-HORSECARS

In 1895 the Citizens converted the bulk of their operations to electric and with the need for many additional cars converted horsecars to electrics. The Detroit Free Press on 11/19/96 reported that of 300 horsecars 67 had been converted, many of the others were auctioned off. The Street Railway Journal in an article in late 1895 covered an inspection visit to the Detroit Citizens's Shops on Jefferson. They reported that a number of 22 foot vestile cars were made over from the old 16 foot cars, three old cars making two new ones. The expense being $260.00 for each car turned out. One car was cut in half and the other two had an end removed between the first and second window. A one-half section was then spliced to the larger section on the other two cars with the small end pieces being thrown away. New floors, new seats, and new sills were required. The new platform was protected with a heavy buffer which took the shape of the vestile protecting the car from damage in case of collision. When the cars were varnished, it was impossible to discover the splice. All cars were mounted on DuPont trucks (note trucks under 464) and equipped with DuPont brakes. These cars were numbered 278-299, (22) and 456-499 (44) a total of 66 cars.

Three views of the ex-horse cars. **TOP: Moore Collection. CENTER: Faber Collection. BOTTOM:** Car 464 out of service in May 1918 awaiting scrapping. **D.U.R. Photo.**

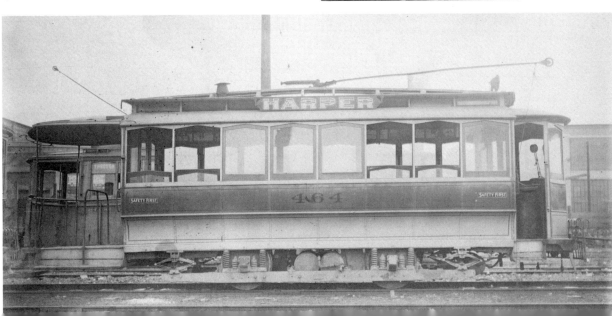

GROUP 6 — THE 1ST GROUP OF D.U.R. BUILT CLOSED CARS

After the takeover, the first item of business was to build 124 single truck cars 34'9" in length, which carried 29 passengers. These cars replaced the 300 series cars on the main 5¢ lines and were the backbone on the fleet. The D.U.R. used numbers open at the time, 51-75, 176, 204-242, 247-271, 300, 392-400. The cars had a plaque in each car reading "Built at Company's Shops".

The cars were fast cars but noisy inside when light. They were built to carry passengers packed in with plenty of standees inside and outside on the large Detroit platform.

TOP: A 1902 shot of car 266 in front of the company shops. **CENTER:** Car 394 shines like new at the end of the 14th line in front of Providence Hospital on West Grand Boulevard. **Schramm collection photos.** **BOTTOM:** Car 74 turns from Hastings onto Forest in 1921. **Manning Brothers Historical Collection.**

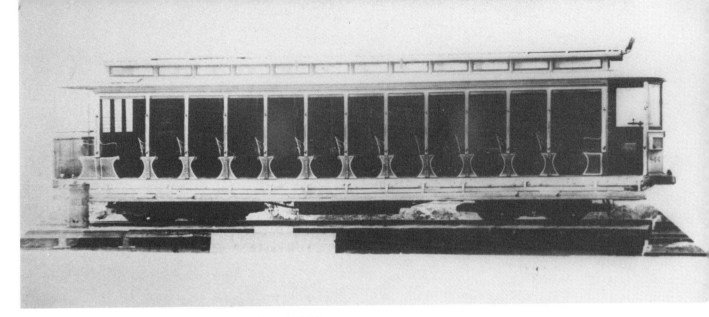

GROUP 7 — THE DOUBLE TRUCK OPEN BENCH CARS 826-846

These cars were originally purchased for suburban service; however, soon transferred to city service on Woodward and Jefferson. In 1911 these cars were rebuilt into closed style city cars with seats arranged parallel to the windows the full length of the car creating a large center isle for standees. The cars were used on Woodward for several years until the 1400's came along then they were sent to various lines such as West Jefferson-Fort etc,. In later years the cars saw service as rush hour trippers especially on the Baker line.

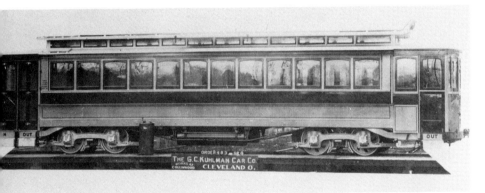

TOP: A Stephenson Builders photo of 14 bench car 844 Detroit's longest and only double truck open car. **CENTER:** Car 841 rebuilt by Kuhlman, this series soon received the nickname "Bowling alley" cars due to their length and wide aisle which allowed for plenty standees. **BOTTOM:** A later photo of 829 taken in Jefferson yard. These were the first P-A-Y-E cars used on the Jefferson line. **Schramm Collection Photos.**

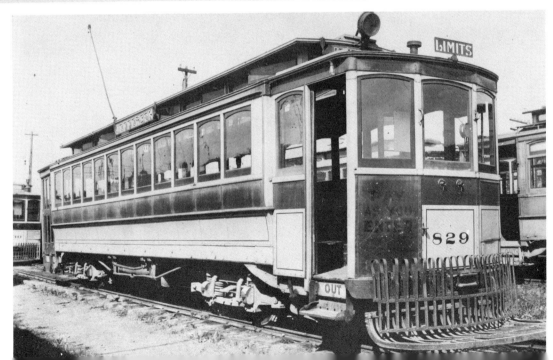

GROUP 8 — THE D.U.R.'S FIRST CLOSED DOUBLE TRUCK CARS.

In 1903 the D.U.R. received these small 40'8" long cars and placed them inservice on the major lines to replace some of their D.U.R. built cars.

In 1916 these cars were converted to P-A-Y-E-type cars and in later years 4 were double ended by the D.U.R. for service on the Stephenson line.

RIGHT: In 1903 the St. Louis Car Company supplied the first closed city double truck 36 seat passenger cars numbered 1028-1052. This photo was taken at the original Baker Car House, at Vernor and Military. **D.U.R. Files. BELOW:** Taken in later years car 1038 still was serving the Baker line and probably at the same car house. **Schramm Collection.**

GROUP 9 — THE D.U.R.'S SECOND GROUP OF DOUBLE TRUCKERS

Evidently pleased with the first double truck cars 1028-1052 the D.U.R. in the next few years placed five additional orders;

		Convert PAYE
1053-1102	built by St. Louis in 1903	1914-15
1103-1152	built by Brill in 1904	1912-14
1153-1177	built by Brill in 1905	1912-14
1178-1202	built by St. Louis in 1905	1912-14
1700-1749	built by Cincinnati in 1907	1909-12
1203-1227	built by Kuhlman in 1908	1912-14

Some comments on these cars;
1053-97 - had St. Louis 47 trucks, balance 27F Brill.

They had 33" cast iron spiked wheels.

1103-1202 - first used on Jefferson and Woodward, fast cars like the 1700's but trucks were noisier than the 050 Standards, good riding and good pick-up.

1203-1227 - Equipped with St. Louis 47 trucks and 2 Westinghouse motors, used on Woodward. Rough riding cars due to type of truck. Car 1211 first car to come with solid wheels.

1700-1749 - original cast iron spoked Davis one wear steel wheels which had a "bell like ring" over the joints and were more quiet running.

These cars were converted to Payee type first by removing the sliding double rear doors. The steps remained open. In later years folding steps and doors were added, and the rear platform enclosed.

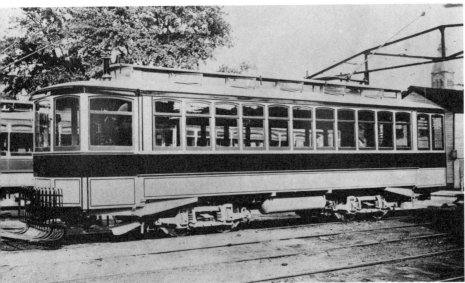

ABOVE: Original appearance of these cars with their open rear platform. **CENTER:** Same car 1116 in later years with rear platform enclosed. **Schramm Collection. BOTTOM:** Interior front of 1715 note interurban advertisement and invitation to read forecoming Electric Service. **Manning Brothers Historical Collection.**

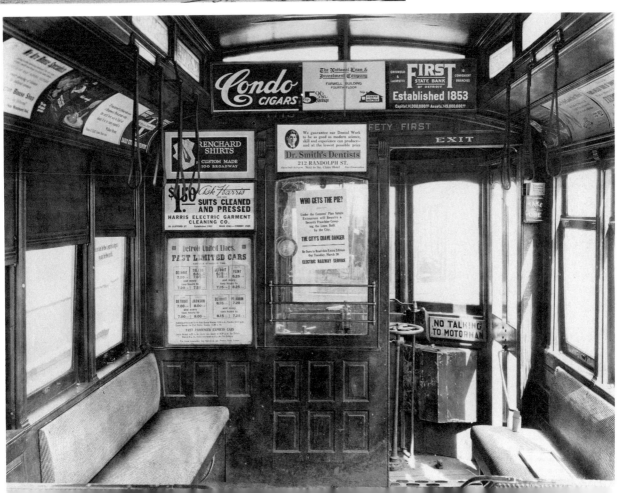

TOP: Car 1722 heading north on Woodward past a new traffic control installation. The first unit was so close to the tracks the interurbans were unable to swing the corner. **Schramm collection.** **CENTER:** Sitting in the Michigan Car Loop after refilling the air tanks. **Schramm Collection. BOTTOM:** Car 1218 going north on Woodward just above Jefferson Avenue showing the enclosed rear platform and crowded street. **D.U.R. files.**

GROUP 10 — THE D.U.R. BUILT CROSS SEAT CARS

After moving to their new shops on Monroe Street the D.U.R. built their second group of closed cars, 1250-1261 in 1905 and 1262-1273 in 1906. These cars were similar in appearance and dimensions, except they seated one more passenger on their cross seats with its side aisle, and had eight windows instead of seven. There is no record of any of these cars being converted to P-A-Y-E operation.

TOP: Car 1264 is in service on the Trumball line. **CENTER:** Another member of this class of cars posses at the end of the Myrtle line at Myrtle and Roosevelt. **Both photos Schramm Collection. BOTTOM:** Car 1260 is at Trumbull Car House in 1910. **Faber Collection.**

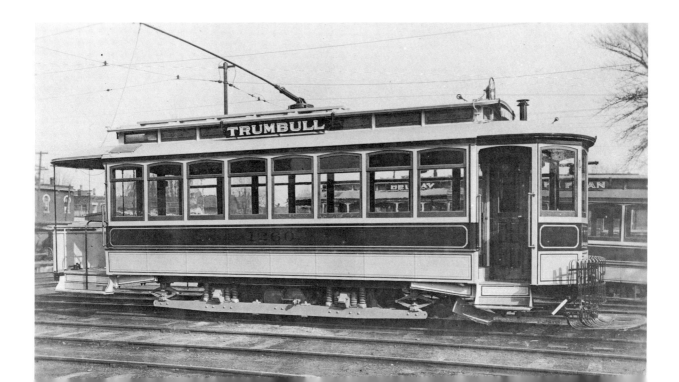

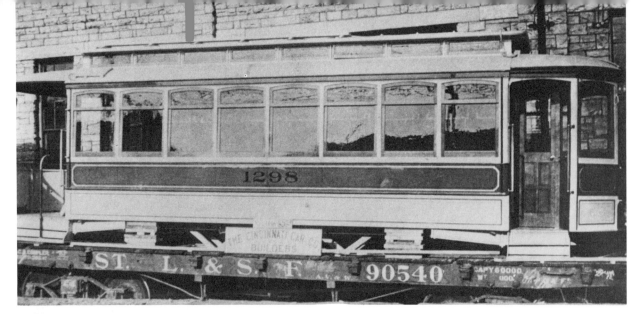

GROUP 11 — THE D.U.R. PURCHASED CROSS SEAT CARS

These single truck cars built by Cincinnati in 1906, were built on the "Kuhlman Pattern" with a side aisle and seated 30. These cars had good speed 30-32 miles per hour and good riding qualities, and were usually assigned to the 3¢ lines. An old employee noted that on the 14th. line when riding them and hitting old track at high speed was like a small boat in a stormy sea.

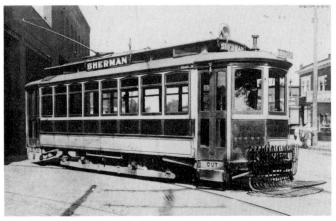

TOP: A builders photo of 1298 prior to shipment by train for Detroit. **D.U.R. Files.**

CENTER: A photo taken at Concord Car House Kercheval and Concord of 1291, this car was the only one known to have been rebuilt as a P-A-Y-E type car and having the rear platform enclosed. **Schramm Collection.**

BOTTOM: This photo taken at time of their scrapping shows the interior of this type car and how the seats and aisle was arranged. **D.U.R. Files.**

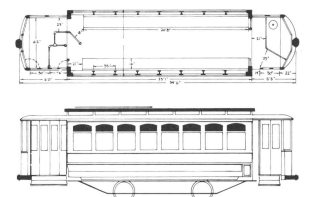

GROUP 12 — THE D.U.R.'S LAST ORDER OF SINGLE TRUCKERS

When the D.U.R. went to Payee type operation the Detroit Railway cars 102-203 were not adoptable. Accordingly they were scrapped (a few kept as work cars) and they were replaced with two groups of cars 900-999 built by American Car Company 1912, and 850-899 built by Cincinnati in 1913. These single truckers took over the 3¢ lines. The motors from the old scrapped cars 102-203 were placed under the new 900 series cars necessitating purchasing only the bodies.

BELOW: Photo was taken at Warren and Lawton showing original appearance of these cars. **RIGHT:** The seats were covered with carpet in the winter while summer patrons sat on just the varnished wood. **Faber Collection.**

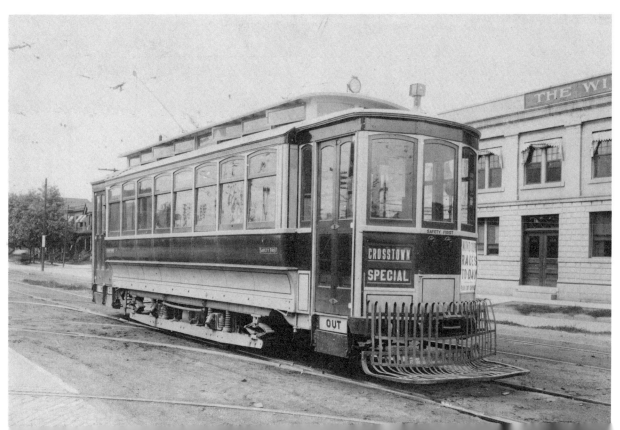

LEFT: A posed photo at the D.U.R. Highland Park Shops, shows 850 after conversion to one-man operation. Note one of the rear doors has been removed to assist in passenger control. **D.U.R. Files. CENTER:** Interior view of car 850 showing the new seating arrangement. The long seat on the right side had been removed and replaced with cross seats making an unusual seating arrangement. This was the only Detroit car series with this arrangement. **D.U.R. Files. BELOW:** A late photo taken showing how this type car looked at time of takeover in 1922. **D.U.R. Files.**

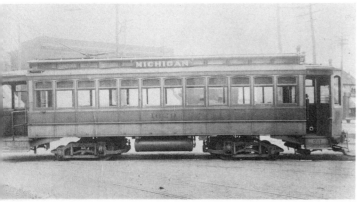

GROUP 13 — THE D.U.R.'S LAST DETROIT PLATFORM CARS

In 1909-1910 the D.U.R. placed four orders,

1775-1799	from Kuhlman in 1909	length 42′3″ seat 43
1750-1774	from Cincinnati in 1910	length 42′3″ seat 43
1625-1649	from Niles in 1910	length 42′2″ seat 43
1650-1699	from Kuhlman in 1910	length 42′2″ seat 43

These were the first payee type cars to operate on Woodward, having folding steps and doors added later. Their speed was 30-33 miles per hour and had Davis steel wheels. These cars were placed on Michigan, Gratiot, Mack and Fort lines.

These cars still retained the small front platform and large rear "Detroit Platform".

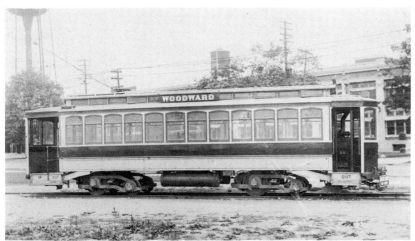

Photos of cars 1629 and 1630 are included since they were the experimental cars along with 1631. **TOP:** 1629 was equipped with double Brill Maximum Traction trucks. **LEFT:** 1630 had double Standard Maximum Traction trucks, and 1631 had double Baldwin Maximum Traction trucks while the rest had double standard trucks. **Schramm Collection. BELOW:** A good early photo of 1768 showing the enclosed rear platform that these cars came with. The folding doors and steps were added in 1917. **Schramm Collection.**

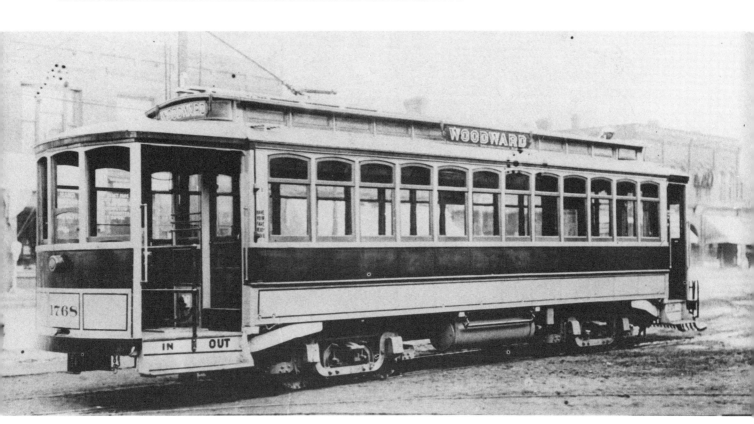

GROUP 14 — THE D.U.R.'S LARGE FRONT PLATFORM CARS.

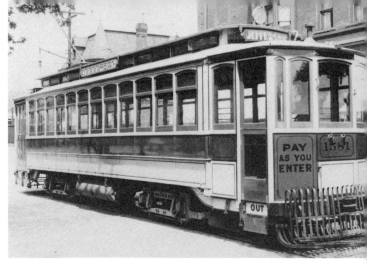

This was the last purchase of wooden body cars by the D.U.R. Also, included in these orders were cars with 4-GE 203 motors to pull trailers and numbered 1375-1474. These cars had smaller rear platforms and larger front platforms to handle Payee type service better.

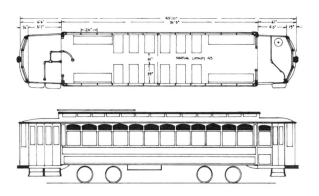

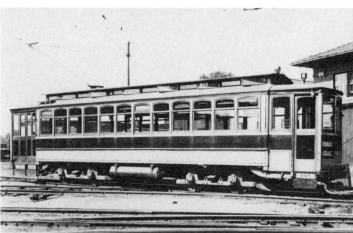

Two photos of 1581 (above) and 1404 (left) showing the folding doors and steps as originally equipped with. **Schramm Collection. BELOW:** An in service shot of 1579 on Woodward. **Manning Brothers Historical Collection.**

GROUP 15 — THE D.U.R. STEEL BODY CARS

The big cars which were needed to handle the large crowds on the major lines, also pulled the large new trailers. The motor cars were purchased from Kuhlman, numbered 3000 through 3099, and had deck roofs. Then in 1918 the D.U.R. built car 3100 with a deck roof, and in 1919 cars 3101 through 3125 with arch roof were built. These cars built at the Highland Park Shops were all four motored with GE 203 motors and were 46'10" in length and seated 46. All except 3109 which had an oil heater, were heated by coal; also, they still used storage air for braking.

The steel body cars were the favorite with the motorman, the 50 H.P. motors, big trucks and high bodies made them excellent snow fighters; their brakes were faster reacting and more powerful than the newer Peter Witts.

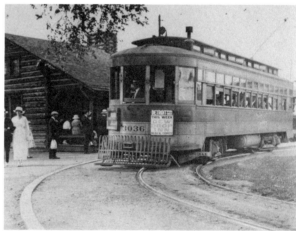

TOP: Southbound Woodward Avenue car 3065 with its trailer in 1920. **Manning Brothers Historical Collection. CENTER:** Car 3036 by the Log Cabin Loop waiting shelter, which was then the end of the City's Woodward line. **Schramm Collection. BOTTOM:** Car 3120. **Dworman collection.**

183

TOP: An interior view of this type car. This photo was taken March 1921. On December 23, 1921, this car was transferred to the M.O. The advertising on the windows was the D.U.R.'s attempts to fight the City takeover and to push their own "service at cost plan". **Manning Brothers Historical Collection. CENTER:** Car 3044 was photographed April, 1920, when the first city proposal to build a competing system was put on the ballot. **Manning Brothers Historical Collection. BOTTOM:** Car 3000 with its trailer passing the old Russel House Hotel. **Schramm Collection.**

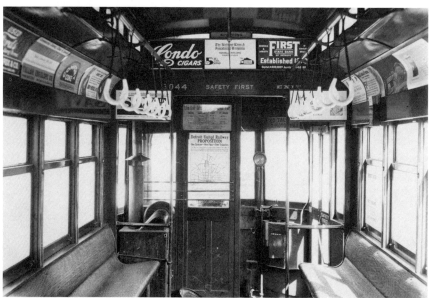

GROUP 16 — THE TRAILERS OF DETROIT

The trailer car was placed in service in Detroit on the Jefferson line shortly after the electric service was introduced. Their use was prompted by several reasons: With the demand for more seats the company could either add an additional motor car with a crew of two; or add a car with a crew of one attached to the motor car. The trailer would cost less, and also utilize the older cars. First the horsecars trailers for the early electrics, then the small early electrics became trailers as they were replaced. This replacement pattern continued until the era of the steel body cars.

Not all lines entering downtown were electrified at first. Therefore, a mixture of fast electrics and slower horsecars caused some early traffic jams. The first attempt to relieve this problem was on the Myrtle line horsecar as it completed its trip downtown. For the Grand River portion of the trip it was attached to the Grand River electric car.

The first cars designed as trailers came in 1915 when the D.U.R. ordered the first large trailers. These trailers were to be pulled by the large steel body 3000 series cars and the wooden body 1400 series cars all equipped with four motors. Both the D.U.R. and the D.S.R. relied heavily on these units to move people on the major lines until replaced by the faster Peter Witts during the 1930's. It should be noted that the traffic carried on these lines had also been substaniately reduced by then due to the depression and the increased use of the private car.

TOP AND BOTTOM: Two photos of trailer 5102 being pulled by 1467 in service on the Grand River line in 1918. **Manning Brothers Historical Collection. ADJACENT PAGE:** Interior of a D.U.R. trailer, this was the standard seating arrangement for these units. This photo of 5032 taken March, 1921, shows the D.U.R. proposals to fight the city takeover. **Manning Brothers Historical Collection.**

GROUP 17 — THE DETROIT BIRNEY'S

The M.O. after promising the citizenry large cars in place of the D.U.R. cars purchased the country's second largest fleet of Birney-single-truck cars. They purchased within a year 250 cars to service their lines even though within a few years they were attempting to sell 200 of them. The cars were derisively referred to as "Couzens Cooties"; and after the purchase of the Peter Witts as "Half-Witts".

OPPOSITE PAGE: Birneys were supplied by various builders from a patent held by Charles O. Birney, but each company had its individual subtle differences built into its model. While the dimensions of the car varied by inches, there were more obvious changes such as roof air vents, window spacing, trolley pole mounts, trucks, door windows, stop lights. The photos on the next page represent cars from the various builders. **TOP LEFT:** St. Louis Car Company (Car 323) **TOP RIGHT:** McGuire-Cummings Car Company (Car 266) **BOTTOM LEFT:** Osgood Bradley Company (Car 112) **BOTTOM RIGHT:** J. G. Brill Car Company (Car 194).

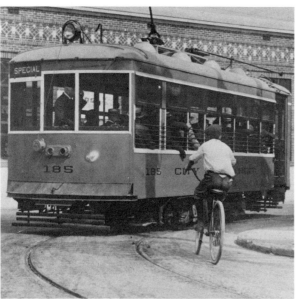

TOP: Builders photo of Birney 150. **CENTER:** August 24, 1921, photograph shows car 185 carrying a load of city officials around a sharp corner at Buchanan and Scotten on a tour. **Both Schramm Collection. BOTTOM:** We had to include one interior photo of a Birney car to show the small space and wooden seats the M.O. offered their passengers after many promises of "large comfortable cars with seats for everyone". **D.S.R. files.**

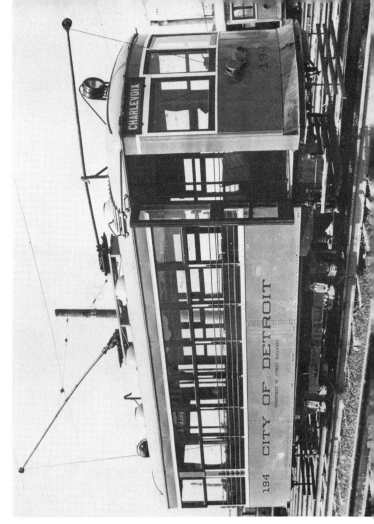

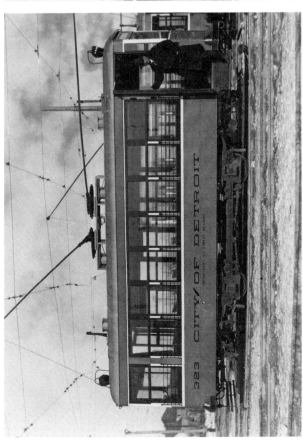

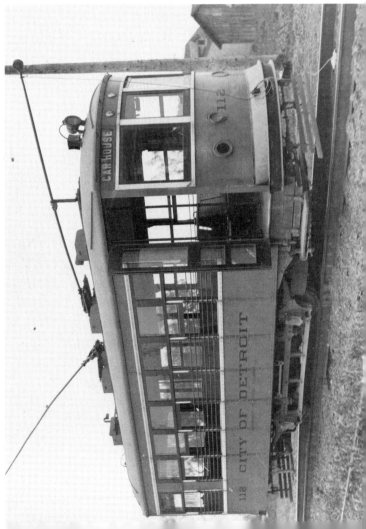

GROUP 18 — THE PETER WITTS

Planning to force the D.U.R. into surrendering some of its major lines such as Woodward and Fort Street, the M.O. purchased 50 large Peter Witts to service these lines. These cars were built by Kuhlman Car Company along general Peter Witt lines; however, the front platform is shorter than usual due to some of the sharp curves and narrow streets on their operating routes.

Originally numbered 1000-1049, they were soon renumbered 11000-11049 when they began opeating joint line service with the D.U.R. who had cars with the same numbers.

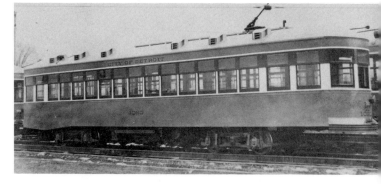

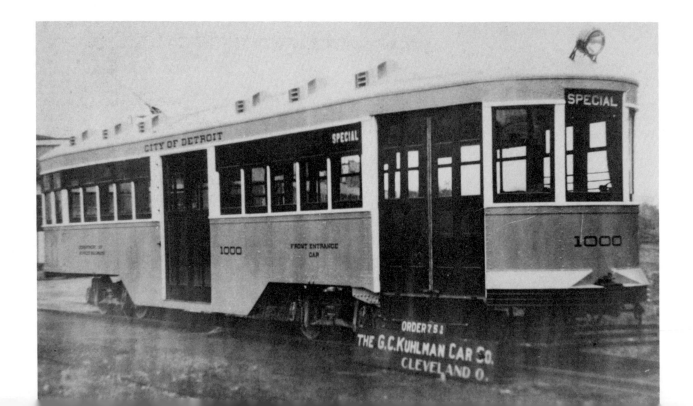

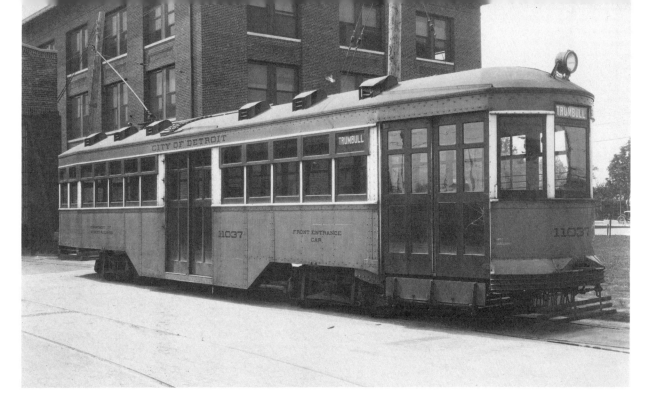

TOP: The numbers were soon changed to keep from conflicting with D.U.R. numbers. Both companies were operating joint service on the Trumbull and several other lines. Accordingly the 1000 series cars became the 11000 series cars. **Schramm Collection. CENTER:** Car 11023 had its front rebuilt from the round style to the square sign style. This new design was specified on all future car orders. **D.S.R. files.**

RIGHT: An accident photo of car 11008 after hitting a dray wagon. Note how far the doors fold out, this caused many collisions with safety zones by forgetful operators. **D.S.R. Files.**

City of Detroit
DEPARTMENT OF STREET RAILWAYS

BULLETIN ORDER

To: Operators and Conductors
Subject: Operation of all City lines by the Dept. of Street Railways, City of Detroit.

General

Effective with the first runs leaving the respective city car houses on the morning of May 15th, 1922, all cars operating on city lines will be the property of the City of Detroit and in charge of city employees.

All platform men in the employ of the City will be classified as follows:

Men in charge of operating one-man and two-man cars will be classified as "Operators".

Men in charge of fare collection on two-men cars and trailers will be classified as "Conductors".

Instructions for the guidance of Conductors and Operators, covering general details of the change of ownership of these lines are given herewith and in addition to these instructions, bulletins will be posted covering specific changes on the various lines.

Equipment

Caps, Badges, Buttons, Rule Books and Punches now in Conductors and Operators possession will be retained by them until further notice.

All refund Slips, Pass Books and Transfers in the possession of Conductors are to be returned to Cashier of the Detroit United Railway at the completion of the day's work on May 14th, or before starting work for the City on May 15th.

Also on joint operation lines, Transfers in the hands of Conductors and Operatiors now in the city employ will be turned in to the Cashier at the completion of the day's work on May 14th.

Conductors will be supplied with a new form transfer and refund slips of the City's issues before taking their runs on May 15th.

Seniority

Conductors and Operators on lines which are now being operated jointly by the City and Detroit United Railway will be placed on the seniority boards in the same position which they held prior to the time that join operation was started. Conductors and Operators on all other lines will hold the same seniority rights with the City as held with the Detroit United Railway.

Working Conditions

Conductors and Operators will receive the same rate of pay as they are now being paid and the same working conditions will remain in force until further notice.

Supervision

The supervision of all lines will be maintained by the present Division Superintendents and their assistants.

Free Transportation

Conductors and Operators in full uniform, Police and Firemen in full uniform, Division Supervising Officials presenting Trackmans Badges will be carried free of charge on City cars. Under no other conditions must a passinger be allowed to ride free on City cars. Conductors and Operators will be held to strict accountability for failure to enforce this rule.

Tickets and Transfer

Free passenger tickets of the Detroit United Railway issue will not be accepted for fare on City cars. Conductors and Operators will accept revenue tickets of the Detroit United Railway issues and revenue tickets (metal tickcto tokens) of the City's issues for payment of fares. TRANSFERS WILL NOT BE EXCHANGED BETWEEN CITY CARS AND INTERURBAN OR OTHER CARS OF THE DETROIT UNITED RAILWAY.

Schedules

New schedules will be placed in effect on certain lines on May 15th, and bulletins covering these schedules have been posted. All other lines will be operated on the same schedules as are now in effect until further notice.

Emergency Calls

All cases of Wire Breaks, Blockades, Derailments, etc., which require the calling of Emergency Apparatus will be handled as in the past- that is, Emergency Calls will be made to the Antoine Station, Telephone Melrose 3240 or Main 2238.

Uniforms

The regulation uniform for both Conductors and Operators of this department will be the same as at present, with the exception that Conductors as well as Operators will be required to wear double brested coats. Conductors will be permitted to wear the uniforms which they now have, until further notice.

During the summer months Conductors and Operators must wear coats at all times, either the regulation blue serge coats or black alpaca coats with the Departments buttons.

E.S. RIDER
Sup't. of Transportation